Reflections

Reflections

Conversations with Politicians

Peter Hennessy and Robert Shepherd

First published in the United Kingdom by
Haus Publishing Ltd
70 Cadogan Place
London SW1X 9AH
www.hauspublishing.com

Copyright © Peter Hennessy and Robert Shepherd, 2016

A CIP catalogue record for this book is available from the British Library

These interviews were first broadcast on BBC Radio 4

ISBN 978-1-910376-48-5
eISBN 978-1-910376-49-2

Typeset in Minion by MacGuru Ltd

Printed and bound in Spain by Liberdúplex

Contents

Acknowledgements

The authors would like to thank: Gwyneth Williams, controller of BBC Radio 4; Mohit Bakaya, commissioning editor, BBC Radio 4; Martin Rosenbaum, executive producer of *Reflections*; our copy editor Paul Coupar-Hennessy; Barbara Schwepcke, founder of Haus publications; and Harry Hall, its managing director.

Introduction

Peter Hennessy

The art of political interviewing

"The historian", wrote EL Doctorow, "will tell you what happened. The novelist will tell you what it felt like."[1] The job of the interviewer is to combine both in the same flight of questioning. It is a craft both intrusive and sensitive, requiring the skills of the inquisitor and the biographer.

In the mid-1980s I took a stab at what I would call 'combat interviewing' of current politicians in a pair of series for Granada Television called *Under Fire*, a revival of a programme pioneered by Robin Day in the mid-'50s. I was wonderfully produced but not altogether at home in the genre, preferring the kind of interviews I was to conduct for 45-minute documentaries as a presenter of the BBC Radio 4 *Analysis* programme.

I am not entirely without aggressive urges but the results of combat interviews can be rather more heat than light – and predictable too. If an interviewer's style is almost all fast-bowling, interviewees will arrive mentally helmeted, padded up and determined to play endless defensive strokes in the manner of the incomparable Trevor Bailey of Essex and England when I was a boy in the 1950s.

Political interviewing of the non-combat variety came late in life, with three summer series of *Reflections* on BBC Radio 4,

---

1 "EL Doctorow", Obituary, *The Times*, 23 July 2015

which began in 2013. The idea belongs to the controller of Radio 4, Gwyneth Williams, and it came to her during a discussion over tea at the Cheltenham Literary Festival in October 2012. The idea was a series of reflective conversations with a degree, one hopes, of bite but not bark – more an interim biography than an excursion into the combat zone, with the occasional burst of 'now it can be told' revelation. To my great delight I was assigned as producer Rob Shepherd, friend over many years and political biographer of repute. The *Reflections* interviewees, I warmly wish, will have many more full and happy years ahead of them, hence the *interim* biographical approach. But there comes a time when a recollective rather than a confrontational conversation is the most fitting and, one hopes, productive approach. Of course, to be candid, there is a feeling, an incentive perhaps, to get the chat in with time to spare. Simon Schama caught it well when he wrote in *Dead Certainties*:

> Historians are left forever chasing shadows, painfully aware of their inability ever to reconstruct a dead world in its complete- ness however thorough or revealing their documentation. We are doomed to be forever hailing someone who has just gone around the corner and out of earshot.[2]

The series have been a great pleasure to make, though tinged with a dash of regret that Rob and I didn't start earlier, for Schama-like reasons, in time to catch several of the now-departed post-1945 generation of politicians, some of whom such as Harold Wilson, Jim Callaghan, Roy Jenkins, Quintin Hailsham, Tony Benn and Enoch Powell I spoke to as part of studio discussions for *Analysis* or in single interviews. Perhaps the greatest challenge would have been a 45-minute conversation with my special politi- cal hero, Clem Attlee, for whom brevity was a way of life. I would

---

2 Simon Schama, *Dead Certainties: Unwarranted Speculations,* (Granta Books, 1991), p320

have run out of questions in five. But how I would have relished it. As for Winston Churchill, it would have been the glorious opposite. I would have been lucky to get four questions in the 45. The stuff of dreams.

Each practitioner comes to the microphone for the first time with ancestral voices and images shaping their approach. Though I did not see the programme as a youngster, political historians and interviewers agree about the broadcast that set the style and tone of interviewing now regarded as standard.

Robin Day himself began his memoir, *Grand Inquisitor*, with the critical moment that changed the British political cosmology:

> The date was Sunday, 23 February 1958. The interview was live. I was sitting in a small studio at Television House, Kingsway, in London. On the other side of the table was the Rt Hon Harold Macmillan MP. TV cameras usually go to Prime Ministers at No 10 Downing Street. On this occasion the Prime Minister had come to the studios, which added to the tension.[3]

The two protagonists were well met, each gifted with their own special histrionics (Day's rasping voice; Macmillan's Edwardian drawl) and props (Day's heavy glasses and spotted bowtie; Macmillan's moustache and slightly seedy, though no doubt once quite expensive, drapery). Both were born actors who liked to create little scenes around themselves.

"As we waited to begin", wrote Day, "the Prime Minister derived considerable amusement from the seating arrangements."

> He drily complained that he was sitting on a hard upright seat, whereas I was enthroned behind the table in a comfortable swivel chair with well-padded arms. This, said the Prime Minister, seemed to 'symbolise the new relationship between politician

---

3 Robin Day, *Grand Inquisitor*, (Weidenfeld and Nicolson, 1989), p1

and TV interviewer'... I offered to change chairs. But the Prime Minister, keeping up the banter, said, 'No. I know my place.'[4]

It was all over in 13 minutes but it shifted both men's careers on to a different trajectory and set a new standard for the style and tone of political interviewing. There were banner headlines on the front pages next morning. As for Macmillan, his official biographer Alistair Horne called it his "first breakthrough as a television personality".[5]

What was novel about the Macmillan–Day encounter? It was the first time a British PM had subjected himself to such an *à deux* interview or faced such vigorous questions courteously but not deferentially put.

It was Day's line of questioning about the future of Selwyn Lloyd, Macmillan's Foreign Secretary, that most excited the newspapers and the political commentariat:

MACMILLAN

Well, I think Mr Selwyn Lloyd is a very good Foreign Secretary and has done his work extremely well. If I didn't think so I would have made a change, but I do not intend to make a change simply as a result of pressure. I don't believe that it is wise. It is not in accordance with my idea of loyalty.

DAY

Is it correct, as reported in one paper, that he would like, in fact, to give up the job of Foreign Secretary?

MACMILLAN

Not at all, except in the sense that everyone would like to give up these appalling burdens which we try and carry.

---

4 Robin Day, *Grand Inquisitor,* (Weidenfeld and Nicolson, 1989), pp1–2
5 Alistair Horne, *Macmillan 1957–86,* (Macmillan, 1989), p149

Day seized the moment with a level of cheek, normal to today's eyes and ears, but shocking by the standards of the 1950s.

DAY

Would you like to give up yours?

MACMILLAN

In a sense, yes, because they are very heavy burdens, but, of course, nobody can pretend that they aren't. We've gone into this game, we try and do our best, and it's both in a sense our pleasure and, certainly, I hope, our duty.[6]

The programme which carried the Macmillan interview, *Tell the People*, soon perished but Robin Day and his style bestrode the world of political interviewing for three decades.

The following year saw the arrival, on the BBC's screens this time, of the second weather-maker interviewer of that era. In my judgement, he's never been surpassed, though he is less well remembered than Robin Day. John Freeman and his *Face to Face* series (1959–62) fused the Doctorow duo – he was partly historian, part novelist and, indeed, part shrink.

Freeman had had what was called a "good war" as a Desert Rat – Montgomery described him as the "best brigade major in the Eighth Army"[7] – and was regarded as among the cream of the fabled Labour intake into the 1945 House of Commons (Churchill wept after hearing his maiden speech saying: "Now all the best men are on the other side"[8]). Freeman rapidly became a junior minister but resigned in 1951. As restless in his professions as he was elusive in his character, he tired of opposition following Labour's

---

6 This exchange is reproduced in Day, *Grand Inquisitor*, p4
7 Hugh Purcell, *A Very Private Celebrity: The Nine Lives of John Freeman*, (Robson Press, 2015), p30
8 Ibid, p62

defeat and was one of the bright young politicos recruited to the BBC by Grace Wyndham Goldie (others included Aidan Crawley, Woodrow Wyatt and Christopher Mayhew).[9]

The idea behind *Face to Face* belongs to its producer, Hugh Burnett, who later said of Freeman: "I wanted him because he was highly skilled at probing closely without causing offence. Walking round the block at Lime Grove [the long-gone ramshackle BBC studios in West London] we discussed the series and the second time round the block he agreed. He also accepted the idea of sitting with his back to the camera, a tiny but important detail that gave rise to a brand new programme format."[10]

From the very first interview of Freeman's, with the famous trial lawyer and judge, Norman Birkett, broadcast on 4 February 1959, *Face to Face* was a critical and popular success. It met Huw Wheldon's description of the BBC's mission as making "the good popular and popular good"[11], and it attracted a huge audience of 4.5 million.[12]

Freeman, himself a rather uncomfortable interviewee of Anthony Clare's in 1988[13], reckoned that, "What was new about it was simply that, for the first time, the interviewer, the camera and the lights and the studio environment were all integrated in a single concentration on the individual who was being interviewed."[14] Freeman's clipped, almost military, voice added to the effect.

The Hennessy family not possessing a television until 1962, the first *Face to Face* I saw was on another family's set in October 1960,

---

9 Charlotte Higgins, *This New Noise: The Extraordinary Birth and Troubled Life of the BBC*, (Guardian Books and Faber, 2015), p82

10 Purcell, *A Very Private Celebrity*, pp138–9

11 Higgins, *This New Noise*, p52

12 Joan Bakewell, 'Introduction', in *Face to Face with John Freeman*, (BBC Books, 1989) p6

13 Purcell, *A Very Private Celebrity*, p2

14 The transcript of the Clare–Freeman interview is reproduced in *Face to Face with John Freeman*, pp9–21

when Freeman's subject was John Reith, first Director-General of the BBC, in the 1920s and 1930s. This huge, granitic figure almost burst out of the screen as he exhibited, under Freeman's ever-courteous questioning, his agonising combination of excessive self-destiny and personal unease. This is the passage that has stayed in my memory from that day to this:

FREEMAN

Lord Reith, tell me how tall you are?

REITH

Six foot six when I stand straight.

FREEMAN

Now, how old were you when you grew to that height?

REITH

About 23.

FREEMAN

Did you at any stage outgrow your strength?

REITH

Never… I've got too much strength, and have had all along, I think.

FREEMAN

Do you look at other people and think, "Well, I'm bigger than he is"?

REITH

No, I usually wish I weren't as big as I am. It's awkward. Anything over six foot two is an affliction, Mr Freeman. Have you got that?

FREEMAN

Yes I have. Would you say of yourself – throughout your life – that you've been an ambitious man?

REITH

Ambition, as normally understood, *absolutely* no. I'm incapable of the techniques which ambition, in the ordinary sense, almost inevitably compels – the devices and expedients that it normally compels. I've been ambitious in this other sense – minded to do whatever came to one's hands with all one's might, both hands; better, to do whatever it was at least as well as anybody else could, and in shorter time. Is that clear? In other words to be fully stretched. Not ambitious for this or that position. Except insofar that this or that position would make one fully stretch, with all one's capacities and intelligence and strength used.

FREEMAN

Can you remember how old you were when you first formulated that thought?

REITH

About 18.

FREEMAN

Was that when you first realised you had great powers of decision and ability to organise others, or were you younger when you first realised that?

REITH

A little bit younger than that.

FREEMAN

Can you remember the occasion vividly, or not?

REITH

Yes. On the top of Ben Macdui in the Cairngorms in Inverness-shire. I had just been climbing and climbing all day long and wondering whatever I was going to do in the world.[15]

And how's this as a coda towards the end of the interview?

FREEMAN

Have you been happy, looking back on your 70 years?

REITH

Oh no.

FREEMAN

You've not be happy?

REITH

No.

FREEMAN

Have you been successful?

REITH

No.

FREEMAN

Well, in what does your lack of success consist, then? I mean, for instance have you ever wanted political power?

REITH

I have wanted to be fully stretched, Mr Freeman, and possibly the

---

15 The transcript of the Reith–Freeman interview is reproduced in *Face to Face with John Freeman*, p128

positions in which one would have been mostly fully stretched are political. Do you want me to be more specific?

FREEMAN

Yes, I would like you to.

REITH

I would like to be have been Viceroy of India. I would like to have been Prime Minister ... But not for the power or patronage, or anything, but for the full stretching.[16]

Freeman conversing with Reith was probably the first proper interview on which I eavesdropped. Quite a place to start.

Freeman and the *Face to Face* series ended when his duties as editor of the *New Statesman* became too time-consuming in 1962, after 35 interviews. But John Freeman's shade – like Robin Day's – lives on. In their different ways, they struck gold first time round and its lustre shines to this day. It would be foolish for any interviewer to contemplate matching either. But there they remain as enduring gilt-edged standards.

Having not a sliver of psychological or psychiatric training, I am wary of invoking Anthony Clare. But the influence of his several series of *In the Psychiatrist's Chair* accumulated such force that I can do no other. Like Freeman, his interviewees were widely drawn and included politicians. Both, for example, interviewed Lord Hailsham. Clare drew from him a fascinating reflection on those who make it to No 10 Downing Street. Hailsham, in a 1989 interview, was asked whether he regretted not winning the Premiership when for a few days in October 1963 he came close to succeeding Harold Macmillan? He replied:

---

16 The transcript of the Reith–Freeman interview is reproduced in *Face to Face with John Freeman*, p134

I've known every prime minister to a greater or lesser extent since Balfour, and most of them have died unhappy... It doesn't *lead* to happiness.[17]

Very true.

Perhaps the greatest British tribute to the interviewer, the interviewer's craft, and the value of the product was when Sir David Frost was admitted to the National Pantheon encased by Westminster Abbey on 13 March 2014, before some 2000 attendees at his memorial service.

The Frost technique ranged through all the keys between his ferocious youth as the front man for *That Was The Week That Was* to his prime position as interviewer of the international good, not-so-good, and occasionally great, with a play and film made out of his legendary interviews with the Watergate-stained former US president Richard Nixon.

It is, of course, impossible for any interviewer to penetrate what Lytton Strachey called "the secret chambers of consciousness"[18] of another person (it's hard enough to scrape the outside of one's own). Yet we all carry an individual identity card in our minds, stamped by a myriad of experiences, hopes, fears, expectations, loyalties and resentments. Perhaps the best an interviewer can hope to do is to access different layers of a personality – what the master pollster Bob Worcester calls opinions, attitudes and values. Values, Bob reckons, are "The deepest of all ... formed early in life and not likely to change".[19] And, of course, an interviewer's own opinions, attitudes and values cannot be entirely set aside during a conversation, however hard he or she may try. This applies too to the best profile writers in the quality press: my palm for

---

17 *In the Psychiatrist's Chair*, BBC Radio 4, 16 August 1989
18 Lytton Strachey, *Queen Victoria*, (Chatto and Windus, 1921), p309
19 Professor Sir Robert Worcester, 'Public Opinion: Friend or Foe?', Chancellor's Lecture, University of Kent, 25 January 2013, p14

this version of the craft practised over many years goes to Terry Coleman of *The Guardian*, closely followed by Susan Barnes of *The Sunday Times*.[20]

For all the perils, the pitfalls and the difficulties, politico-historical interviewing will remain for me a thing of fascination and possibility. I admire and salute those who subject themselves to it. The 11 caught between these covers have my gratitude for agreeing to be interviewed and for permitting their transcripts to be reproduced.

20 Terry Coleman, *The Scented Brawl: Selected Articles and Interviews*, (Elm Tree Books, 1978); Terry Coleman, *Movers and Shakers: Conversations with Uncommon Men*, (Andre Deutsch, 1987); Susan Barnes, *Behind the Image*, (Cape, 1974)

Shirley Williams (Baroness Williams of Crosby)

Series 1, Episode 1, first broadcast 11 July 2013

Born 27 July 1930. **Educated** St Paul's School
for Girls; Somerville College, Oxford

MP (Labour) Hitchin 1964–79; Hertford and
Stevenage 1974–79; (SDP) Crosby 1981–83

Parliamentary Secretary, Ministry of Labour 1966–67; Minister
of State, Department of Education and Science 1967–69; Minister
of State, Home Office 1969–70; Secretary of State for Prices and
Consumer Protection, 1974–76; Secretary of State for Education and
Science, 1976–79. Deputy Leader, Liberal Democrats, House of Lords,
1999–2001; Leader, Liberal Democrats, House of Lords, 2001–2004.

Autobiography *Climbing the Bookshelves*, 2009

HENNESSY

With me today is that rarity: a politician with a gift for inspiring considerable respect across the parties, and a high degree of affection among the public, even when she espouses policies that do not inspire universal hosannas of approval. She's also a collector's item for being, over the span of her career, a powerful player in no less than three political parties: Labour, the SDP, and now the Liberal Democrats. Shirley Williams, welcome.

WILLIAMS

Thank you.

HENNESSY

Shirley, you belong to a generation whose opinions were powerfully shaped by the Second World War and the events that led up to it, the slump and so on. When you went up to Oxford in 1948, do you think you were pretty well formed, as both a character and a political character, by then?

WILLIAMS

Yes, I was born into a world where dreams were possible. It was a wonderful world. The war had been rough and tough, but at least it had broken down a lot of the old social class barriers, so that in the air-raid shelters or on the Tube you met a lot of people you wouldn't have met normally if it was the old middle-class structures of the 1920s and the 1930s, which were awful. That was the first thing that made me feel that I was somehow involved with people as a whole; I was one of them and they were part of me.

The second thing was an extraordinary sense of possibility. That was partly the nature of the Attlee government, which was absolutely full of stars, and what was brilliant about Attlee was he was a great cosmologist who could organise all these stars and get them to more or less work together. Most of them were driven by a really genuine wish to build a new society, they weren't there to get the odd sort of lobby position or anything of that kind, those things were rather rare at that time. So that was also very exciting: if you were a young person you could feel real commitment to your government, a real feeling of identification with it.

And the third thing I think was that we were plunged into a world which was no longer imperial but was very international. So great moments, like the sudden independence of India – and my family, which had been much involved in India, knew Pandit Nehru, knew some of the great figures like that – you suddenly realised you were entering into a completely new world, and a wonderful one.

So for all those reasons I remember having a feeling of almost total joy, and almost total compatibility when I got to Oxford, and that drove me through my three years in Oxford, which I found immensely satisfying, and very joyous. One of the reasons for that, I should add, is that of course about two-thirds of the men at Oxford – and there were very many men and very few women, one in eight were women – had gone through part of the war or all of the war, they were people who had been matured by their experiences and by the challenges they experienced. So it was to go to a very grown-up university, it wasn't a university which felt like an extension of school, as I'm afraid often they did, and do still, it was a university which was addressing the problems it was going to have to confront as it got out into the world outside the military forces, and that was also wonderful.

HENNESSY

I think you once said that the Attlee revolution was about the only revolution you could think of that hadn't devoured its own children.

WILLIAMS

[*Laughing*] Yes, that's correct! Indeed, far from devouring them, it actually gave them orange juice and various kinds of vitamin oils.

HENNESSY

I know you're a very optimistic person, but do you think you've been trying to replicate that glorious moment ever since? In many ways, because of the duress of Hitler, and the shared privations of the Home Front – an enormously well-organised Home Front for public purposes and warfare purposes – and the Beveridge Report, a new welfare system, and all the rest of it coming through, it's been downhill for one of nature's social democrats like you? You've had to live with many disappointments on the road from 1945 ...

WILLIAMS

That's true. I'm not somebody who spends a lot of time looking backwards; I hardly reminisce at all. I find when I wake up I think about what's going to happen this week, next week, years from now, but not much about where I was then. However, having said that, yes, there's something in what you say. I think in a sense, social democracy – which was a wonderful political movement – has probably almost reached the end of its potential. Why? Mainly because of globalisation. I was talking at a breakfast for doctors and medical people, and one of the things we discussed was whether the fashion for equality – equality of attitude and of status, very much part of a lot of legislation today – was no longer being applied to wealth and income. It was as if the feeling was that you couldn't do that, you couldn't get there. So we're looking at hugely growing inequalities, which I find extraordinarily painful to think about, and I suspect they're there as long as we don't come up with international answers. One example: I'm very strongly in favour of people dealing with things like tax avoidance, and all the rest of it; the trouble is, if you only have six tiny tax havens, you have the means of escaping from what democratic national governments can do. And I think it's taken me some time to think through how one could actually bring back social democracy, but it would have to be an international and no longer a national movement.

HENNESSY

Going back to the high water of those times, the 'never again' impulse, 'never again slump and war', the powerful motivation for your generation ... What about the politicians who you got to know through your remarkable mother, Vera Brittain, and your wonderful father, George Catlin? I mean you had a household in which the Herbert Morrisons of this world would quite naturally come through. You had great figures from the Labour movement who you knew from being a young girl, and who talked to you.

WILLIAMS

[*Laughing*] I think they felt it as an obligation to be nice to the child, the way you do, or did in those days. But I certainly remember meeting people like George Lansbury, who was a marvellously ideal figure, I mean somebody who was completely wrapped up in equality and peace and tolerance, and every good thing you could think about – but was not, perhaps for that very reason, a completely effective politician. I remember people like Herbert Morrison and Ernest Bevin being very dismissive of George Lansbury, who was the leader of their own party. The second thing, I think, was that we met a large range of people from what was still called the empire. It was just stopping being the empire, so they were people like Chief Lutuli from South Africa, and of course Nehru as I earlier mentioned, his sister, Mrs Pandit, and so forth – we met them all, and I think therefore that I imbibed from a very early age the feeling that the human race comes in rainbow colours, and that was terribly important. I didn't even have to think about it. The other thing I didn't have to think about as a result of my childhood was what I learned later, rather painfully, which was that, like it or not, women had for a very long time been seen as the second sex, and still to a great extent are. And I find as I get older, I get more and more irritated, when I try to take part in the conversation and I'm simply not there, and it's still true.

HENNESSY

Even now? Even for you?

WILLIAMS

Even now, even for me. But it's certainly diminished; it's not quite as universal as it used to be. But it's still there, sometimes.

HENNESSY

There was one side effect of this which you were very candid about in your memoir. You had a tendency to defer to men, right through, to some degree, not just these handsome young men back from the forces and so on, but Roy Jenkins your great friend, and perhaps Jim Callaghan and Harold Wilson too. You criticised yourself for being rather prone to thinking that the men are the big ones …

WILLIAMS

I think it was actually more manipulative than that. I learned early on that it was very difficult to get men to pay any serious attention to a woman who was a great deal younger than themselves. I learned therefore that the way to get their attention, and that didn't mean their physical or sexual attention, their intellectual attention, was in effect to be rather polite to them. Even sometimes a bit grovelling, you might say, when I was very young. And I found that there were very few men who were prepared to accept one's equality right away. One of those very few was Harold Wilson. I've always held Harold Wilson in quite high esteem because he was almost, I think, the only Prime Minister I've ever met for whom gender, religion and colour were totally irrelevant. He only minded about whether you were a decent politician, an able minister, and of course he wanted you to be a supporter of *him*, that's understandable, that's universal – but not on the grounds of race, colour or religion. He really didn't take any notice of them. And I think that was remarkable.

HENNESSY

You once came up with a wonderful piece of anthropology about the place of women in politics. I think you said that the men are only happy if they can categorise you into the dragon, the sexpot, the carer, or the chum.

WILLIAMS

That's correct. And I chose 'the chum' because that's the safest.

HENNESSY

And you were the chum, deliberately the chum.

WILLIAMS

I was deliberately the chum. I saw one or two of my colleagues fall on their swords in the pursuit of being sexpots, that's absolutely hopeless, no future in being a sexpot at all; for one thing you're going to get older, and you'll be an unsuccessful and unsatisfactory sexpot once you pass the age of about 45 or 50, which is exactly when you're likely to get positions of responsibility in politics, in the Cabinet or wherever. The chum thing was the easiest; for one thing it gave me a sort of non-sexual relationship to men, so I could be part of a group, which I often was. I remember being part of the Hattersley-Walden group very early on, after I first got into Parliament. The other thing I didn't much fancy was of course the sort of maternal roles, which was also part of what one might be. I think it was mostly the media that tended to see one in this light.

HENNESSY

The Education ministry, Social Security, those were the sort of jobs for senior women politicians?

WILLIAMS

Well, of course, and health.

HENNESSY

And health.

WILLIAMS

And what I longed for was something that was not typecast as a woman's job. Because I had a job at the *Financial Times* when I came into Parliament, I remember my maiden speech was about international financial relations. That's because I didn't want to be typecast as a 'woman's job' woman, and although I tried very hard to struggle away from that, of course I did actually end up with two almost archetypal women's jobs: Prices, and Education and Science, less so. Those two.

HENNESSY

They were your Cabinet-rank jobs.

WILLIAMS

They were my Cabinet-rank jobs, and they were what one might see as being the outstanding women's jobs.

HENNESSY

It could be an advantage though, Shirley, this chum side. I remember – leaping ahead a bit, to the mid-70s when Labour comes back with no majority in '74 – I was on *The Times* and my friend Ronald Butt, who was the conservative commentator on *The Times*, wrote a piece about you saying that it's not a particularly exciting government and the country's ill-at-ease with itself; but Mrs Williams is exempt from this, because she gives impressions to a wide swathe of people – and this is her appeal – that politics isn't the be-all and end-all for her, and she comes to a political meeting as if it were in-between bottling the fruit. That's what he said; it's always stuck with me. And it's sort of faintly patronising, but at the same time, he's on to something isn't he? That 'Shirley the Chum' meant Shirley who could embrace a large chunk of the political spectrum, albeit from left of centre.

WILLIAMS

Well, it's nice of him; I don't think it's quite accurate. First of all, I can't bottle fruit, I've never even tried. I'm not a bad cook, but bottling fruit, no, and for that matter, tapestry, no. Secondly, we should always add another bit to me, which of course relates to the theatre. I tried to be an actress at one time – I was an actress at one time – and I love reading poetry, and I love reading literature. And of course, because of my mother, I had a lot of links to authors. So I don't think it's quite right.

HENNESSY

But you were within an inch of becoming a world-famous Hollywood star, weren't you? Because when you were in America, evacuated in Minnesota for the first few years of the war, you were very close to becoming *National Velvet*, weren't you? The Elizabeth Taylor slot, that made Elizabeth Taylor the starlet she was and look what that led to.

WILLIAMS

Not just a starlet, but then the star! Well indeed, well what did it lead to: it led to seven husbands, which I think would have been very tiring; it led to a lot of jewellery, which I feel I would certainly lose, and not be able to find again; and I always thank God I didn't get the job!

HENNESSY

Going back to those big figures in the Labour party after the War; Clem Attlee was very hard to get to know; as Douglas Jay famously said, he never used one syllable where none would do. Very hard to chat with, Clem Attlee, I would imagine. But I think on one occasion you got him out of a hole, didn't you? Wasn't it some grand eastern district Labour Party conference in the 50s when you were a young candidate?

WILLIAMS

Yes, he was being terribly boring about China. I think he'd decided to be sort of semi-academic, so he was talking for something like 50 minutes about China, which was not really very high in the salience of most British voters at that time, so the chairman slipped me a note which simply said, 'For God's sake, do something', because by this time, the East Anglian ladies were doing something which you always did when you weren't listening to the speaker, which was to start knitting. And there was a front row which consisted of East Anglian ladies, all knitting.

HENNESSY

Clackety clacking!

WILLIAMS

Quite loud, yes. So I thought, well I've got to do something. Luckily, I had a friend, Val Arnold-Forster … she was an intern in Parliament, she spent her time digging out people's waste-paper baskets, and she'd found in one waste-paper basket, in Attlee's office, a poem, which she handed me, and I thought, in desperation, I'll read that poem out. And I remember, it went like this: *In Limehouse, in Limehouse, before the break of day, I hear the feet of many men that go upon the way, That wander through the city, The grey and cruel city, Through streets that have no pity, Through streets where men decay.* It was a tribute to his time at Toynbee Hall, and of course what it said suddenly was, this is a man of very strong emotions, who isn't going to express them to you, who's going to keep them to himself, who's an officer and a gentlemen, and therefore very short in what he said. But underneath all that is this deep socialist heart, beating away, and the audience went up in rapture. They were so thrilled that afterwards the Chairman said, would you like to meet Mr Attlee? And I said, 'That would be wonderful'. So we went down. And I'd said that the poem was written in 1912. And all Attlee did was look at me and say, '1911, actually'. [*Hennessy laughs*]

WILLIAMS

And that's all he said.

HENNESSY

But you'd silenced the knitters …

WILLIAMS

I'd silenced the knitters, but not aroused Mr Attlee.

HENNESSY

Harold Wilson brought you on very quickly. You win Hitchin in 1964, and Labour comes back with a very small majority. But Harold, within a few years, makes you a junior minister, and also obviously rated you very highly because you were one of the most rapidly promoted of the new intake, weren't you?

WILLIAMS

That's true; but it's also true that he wanted to make a point, that 'I'm open to young people of ability regardless of their sex'. And that was quite an important part of it. I think he would have probably promoted me somewhat slower if I hadn't been a woman. It was an advantage, not a disadvantage.

HENNESSY

I think too, you've very nearly resigned quite early on, didn't you, over the Kenyan Asians.

WILLIAMS

Harold Wilson once said to me that one of his backbench colleagues came to him and said, 'Shirley Williams will probably resign on this issue'. He said, 'That's all right, I've got a wardrobe full of resignation letters.'

HENNESSY

From you? You'd actually sent him a lot of resignation letters?

WILLIAMS

Not lots, but about four. One of the big ones was as you rightly say the East African Asians. I just couldn't stomach that. I thought it was completely absurd to break the promise that had been made to them quite openly by Duncan Sandys, who was Commonwealth Secretary, and by Iain Macleod, who was the Colonial Secretary, and both these men had gone out at the time of Kenyan Independence, and made an absolute pledge that anyone – probably a Kenyan Asian, presumably a Kenyan white also – who wanted to come to Britain, had the right of abode here. And that meant they couldn't be stopped by the Home Office, who like stopping people coming anywhere. So they then broke it. At least Macleod did not break it, but Duncan Sandys openly broke it and said, 'We can't possibly consider these people'. And I remember Jim –

HENNESSY

Jim Callaghan was Home Secretary.

WILLIAMS

Yes, and I think he felt two things, really. One was – it was the immediate aftermath of Powell making his 'Rivers of Blood' speeches – so he certainly feared the possibilities of a really major racial clash in the main towns of England, particularly the north of England. And secondly he thought it was bad politics. I was very angry with him. I thought, we have made an obligation, we have a promise, we've got to make it to these people. But I then said to Jim, look, you won't agree to having a whole lot right away; may I suggest we ask people to queue a bit, and I will go to India, and see the Foreign Secretary, and ask him if he will allow people to queue in India, who would then move in a year or two, when things had calmed down, to England. And he said, well you can do what you like. So I went to India, and I saw the Foreign Secretary, Swaran Singh, and I always remember he said, 'Oh, that's quite all right, my dear. We're such a big country we'll hardly notice them, but you have to keep your promise over the next few years'. And I came back triumphant, with the feeling that at least I'd made some difference. And I think over the next three or four years almost all the East Africans who wanted to come, particularly those from Uganda, managed to get here, and ever since then I felt terribly pleased about that particular aspect of my career.

HENNESSY

I think you liked being a Minister. Most of the senior civil servants always enjoyed working with you. And you enjoyed working with them.

WILLIAMS

I did, I like civil servants. I'm passionately against Francis Maude's mad idea of letting ministers appoint their own civil servants, because frankly I've seen America and although there are many things about America I admire, one of the worst things is the appointment of the first two or three layers down, because it means you begin to lose any sense of what it is to be part of a national community, and you don't get the right advice. Because you've appointed them you get advice which you want to hear.

HENNESSY

So it would end speaking truth under power, which is the great tradition of British Crown Service.

WILLIAMS

Well, it's not always unmitigated truth, but it's a sort of … civil-service truth, which is not quite the same thing. But it does mean they will actually say to you, 'Excuse me, minister, this won't go down well, or this will not work, or we can't bring this about, or we can't deliver it', and I respect that. I think they are very good, and frankly I'm very sad to see the way in which special advisers are beginning to replace civil servants at the top, because I think special advisers, with a few exceptions where there is a great technical issue, such as with nuclear weapons, are basically not a good idea. I'm sorry, I'm very old-fashioned about that. I think, experts, yes, and I think, advisers maybe; but special advisers whose full-time job is advising, and then taking over from the minister – not much democracy, in my view.

HENNESSY

Can we talk a little bit about personal life, because by the time the Labour government fell in 1970, you'd risen rapidly through the ranks with a tremendous workload, and yet you were a young mother, and you were married to the brilliant philosopher Bernard Williams, who I only met once or twice but who was the most captivating, mercurial man.

WILLIAMS

Yes.

HENNESSY

Riveting to talk to.

WILLIAMS

He was like an intellectual dragonfly, every colour you can imagine, and he hovered around ideas, picking them up beautifully. He was an astonishing man.

HENNESSY

But I think you described in your memoir how 1970 was your year of catastrophe, the government fell and your marriage broke up. The price politicians pay in terms of family life can be immensely high and that year is searing on the page in your memoir.

WILLIAMS

It's still searing in my life. I was devoted to Bernard, he was a sort of tremendously colourful personality, tremendously attractive to women, and he didn't always find that resistible. I couldn't really blame him, he fell in love with somebody else, and he genuinely fell in love with them. But it was very tough. I remember it was very tough on my child, and it was very tough on me. And of course if you're a woman, you are particularly exposed. The media are fascinated, to this day, by women politicians and particularly by women politicians' private lives. You would see journalists sitting in trees when you drove home, and you'd see them poking about your garden when you tried to go into your house. And in some cases, which was worse, sitting at the school wall, asking teachers how my child was getting on, and how she was reacting to all this and so forth. So, no, it is very tough, there's no doubt about it, and it's not getting easier – it's probably getting worse.

HENNESSY

The 70s become increasingly tough politically for you, too. The European virus begins to eat deeply into the Labour party. It's been the Conservative party recently that's been three yards away from nervous breakdown on Europe, but in the 70s it was your party. And Roy Jenkins resigned over the referendum question and so on … it was all very tough. And at the very moment we went into the Community in 1973 … it's been one of the great motivators for you in life, in your political life –

WILLIAMS

Oh yes. Absolutely.

HENNESSY

I remember seeing the old film of Harold Macmillan on your arm, on the very day we entered the Community in January '73, going across Parliament Square with young people there celebrating.

WILLIAMS

With bonfires. It was just like the First World War. Bonfires all over Parliament Square, made by the young people with screwed-up newspapers and things of that kind. And I remember Harold Macmillan sniffing the air which smelled unusually of bonfires, of burning wood, and I could see him literally move from my eyes back to Arras and Mons and away from Parliament Square, and you could suddenly see how the whole story of his life had culminated in this moment: when at long last the First World War and the Second were going to be put for ever behind us all. And it was, for him, a kind of renaissance almost, a sort of rebirth.

HENNESSY

I think he said, 'Never again, never again' to you, didn't he, as he walked across the square.

WILLIAMS

He did, he did. Not as a question. As a statement.

HENNESSY

No more war – Europe's cracked it in that sense. Looking back, Shirley, your generation did sing a song of Europe. You always have sung a song of Europe. And yet, here we are, deeply scratching at ourselves, the emotional deficit with Europe is absolutely palpable. I mean, who knows how a referendum will turn out, if indeed we have one in the next few years. But that song of Europe, it isn't the dominant strain any more, is it, within the national family. It just isn't. That must be a real pain for you.

WILLIAMS

I think it's a pain both ways. First of all, one has to say that the Europe we were talking about is not quite the same Europe we have now. The coming in – in a way a wonderful achievement – of the whole of Eastern Europe into the European Union was the culmination of the whole idea of a united Europe. On the other hand it brought with it people who had rather shaky ideas of what democracy means, not very strong senses of accountability – look at Hungary, and look at, for example, Bulgaria. It became almost entirely an economically centred community; that was partly, I'm afraid, Mrs Thatcher, who was only prepared to go ahead on the single market, and really never saw the point of political union, and that undermined any move towards democracy. And I have to be honest and say also that the Commission no longer has as its stars – rather like what you were saying about the Attlee government of 1945 – men and women who are capable of reaching out across the whole of the continent, and giving people a sense of belonging to that continent. Whereas I think when you look back to people like Brandt, or Schmidt, or for that matter Delors, you're looking at great men, and I would say one or two great women too, who have passed from the scene, who had a really huge vision.

For me, I think the other side of that is the United Kingdom itself. It's always had a lasting sickness about no longer being the head of the empire, which has been brilliantly handled by the Commonwealth concept and the Queen and all the rest of it … brilliantly handled. But because it's been so brilliantly handled, we've never really quite faced up to the fact that we're no longer a great power, and we *are* no longer a great power – we can only be an influential power if we are part of a bigger unit than ourselves.

HENNESSY

So you think there's an emotional overhang from the imperial days, the great-power days, indeed superpower days, in some people's memory.

WILLIAMS

I do. It does mean that people still, particularly older people, find it hard to adjust to Britain's actual position, and to recognise, to put it bluntly, that if we actually walk out of the European Union, in my view we will count for almost nothing. We will go to the edges of the football ground, and be watching and shouting and no doubt barracking, but we won't be part of the match. I think that's terribly dangerous, because I think there are real contributions that Britain can make, and I think Britain as a country will eat its heart out if it has no international role any more. It's a country like France, which has an international sense. But if we go out of it, we're going to be a bad-tempered, small, deeply disappointed country.

And one other thing to say: I travel a lot, as you know, and when I've gone to places like China, South Africa, the United States – all three are totally puzzled about why we should think of getting out of the European Union. They understand the Euro-zone was badly handled. It was a foolish ideal; it might have worked if they had laid down conditions at the beginning, but they never did, so they have the Greeces and the Spains coming in without beginning by saying, 'These are the things you have to achieve before you can come in'. All that was a big mistake, but it's not a reason to get out of the Union. The Union still stands there, and I think it's absolutely critical. And I think therefore that the attitude of quite a lot of people, particularly the right-wing of my sister party over there, in the coalition, really have got it terribly wrong, and I wouldn't even say any more – which really is painful – that the idea of any kind of conflict within the European Union itself is completely unthinkable. And that was certainly true for 50 years, a good long time to not have any wars in the Union part of Europe.

HENNESSY

Going back to Labour in the 1970s. You become Secretary of State for Education. Labour has very strong views on comprehensive schools, and you've been a great supporter of comprehensive schools. Do you not think they should have been more of an experiment, rather than the single model? Some of them became very big, certainly in urban areas, with the ending of streaming for example in many of them, and the ladder of opportunity for working-class kids, grammar-school kids, was considerably diminished. That's the criticism of what you did as Education Secretary, as you know.

WILLIAMS

Yes, OK, well first of all, I promoted the idea of a core curriculum, but not the complete curriculum, which Mr Gove has today. In other words about 50% of the comprehensive school would be devoted to key subjects like Maths, English Literature and English Language and so forth. But the other 50% – which is *much* more than today, much more – would be a matter for the school to promote and put forward what they thought was a proper curriculum for the kinds of kids that went to their school, for the kind of areas in which they lived, and so forth. In other words it retained a certain element of closeness to local authority. I didn't and don't agree with the idea of flinging the local authorities out altogether; I think it means you have, in the end, much more uniform kinds of schools than you would have had if you'd retained them, and I deeply disagreed with Ken Baker, in the 1988 Act.

HENNESSY

With his great Education Reform Act.

WILLIAMS

The great Education Reform Act, which booted the local authorities virtually out completely. I think that was a big mistake, and oddly enough, it doesn't fit very well with 'localism' as a concept. I secondly thought – apart from the idea of only a core curriculum, not a total curriculum – I also retained and fought for the right of schools to choose to be single-sex rather than co-educational, thinking partly of the arrival of our friends, the Muslims from East Africa. Most of them would not have sent a girl to a co-educational school at that time.

HENNESSY

And Asia too, not just East African Muslims.

WILLIAMS

No, of course not, so that's just one example. I very strongly believe therefore that people should be able to opt for single-sex. I believe that we should retain the church schools, the faith schools, as another alternative, including, if they want it, Muslim and Jewish schools. I believe there should be a good deal of autonomy for the schools, but not the kind of autonomy we've got today. I have to say I'm very, very dubious about the academy experiment, partly because I think it will almost inevitably lead back to selection in some form or other, not necessarily exam selection, but other kinds of selection. And on the third point: yes, of course it's true that there were some brilliant direct-grant schools, and one or two very good grammar schools, which is why places like Durham didn't want to go to comprehensive very much.

HENNESSY

Which is a Labour authority …

WILLIAMS

It's a Labour authority, yes. But the sheer number of youngsters today who went to comprehensive schools and who have come up to me at opera houses and choral schools and technical laboratories and so on, and said, 'I went to comprehensive school and now I *am* X, Y, Z', always makes me feel that it was right, because people tend to forget two things. One was that in most counties or shire education authorities, not more than about one child in eight or 10 ever went to grammar school.

HENNESSY

Some were higher: a quarter.

WILLIAMS

Some were. But some were even lower. I mean if you look at some of the Midland schools, you'd be lucky to get nine or 10% going to a grammar school. None of them I think exceeded 25%. And the other critical statistical point to make is that the transfer of youngsters who emerged from their primary school and began to blossom to grammar schools was tiny. One and half, one per cent a year. So, really, an awful lot of youngsters simply didn't have an opportunity, and I thought they should have, and I think they've actually made a great deal out of that opportunity.

Now, add two things to that: one is, we've never gone for the kinds of really advanced forms of training of teachers like that, for example, in a totally comprehensive country like Finland, now the best in the whole of the OECD world, by quite a wide margin over all other countries: totally comprehensive. But what they've done is to put their money into getting their teachers up to an MA or even a DEd status. Being a teacher in Finland is a very impressive thing to be. We've squabbled, we've fought, we've had divisions between unions and the executive – but we've never really given teachers the status that they ought to have. And even now, with Mr Gove, the status goes to the headteacher, but it doesn't really go to the teacher. And that's where you really need to have in-service training and all the rest of it, to make the teacher a very special person.

HENNESSY

The Labour government, in which you were a very senior Cabinet minister by the end, you chaired all sorts of Cabinet committees as well as doing the Education job, ended in the wreckage of the Winter of Discontent and a Labour civil war that was already under way before the government fell, and Mrs Thatcher came in. In the civil war again you were in the epicentre, because you were on the national executive committee of the Labour Party, where it was fought out in brutal terms.

WILLIAMS

Correct!

HENNESSY

It must have been absolutely frightful.

WILLIAMS

It was perfectly horrid. Quite a lot of the time the national executive was directed primarily against poor old Jim Callaghan, who I actually think was quite a good Prime Minister, and quite a popular Prime Minister, and actually ran miles ahead of the party in the 1979 general election, a fact that the far left didn't take too much notice of. But he was put up almost as a cockshy; a lot of the executive motions were directed against the previous Labour government, almost as if it would have been better not to have had it. The other thing that was very central, and I think completely crazy, was the concept of the Trade Union Advisory Committee. I would say exactly the same thing, by the by, about big banks today. I don't think that major groupings in a society should have the ability to dictate to government what it should do. Of course they get to try to influence it.

HENNESSY

Trade Union power was excessive by the end of '79, you think?

WILLIAMS

Oh yes, much earlier than that, because you had the Trade Union Advisory Committee, which actually looked at every piece of legislation that was about to be put forward.

HENNESSY

That was 1974, yes.

WILLIAMS

And that was Wilson's attempt to try and keep them on board. But it was constitutionally, I think, very bad. And I would say exactly the same thing the other way round: you've got the influence of banks and big manufacturing and so on. And I could see that Labour was destroying its electoral base, and beginning to actually open the door to attitudes which had very little to do with democracy.

HENNESSY

But it tore into you, leaving the Labour party, because you loved it, didn't you. I think you said it was like drawing your own teeth.

WILLIAMS

It was, yes.

HENNESSY

I think you and Bill Rodgers of the four (with David Owen and Roy Jenkins) were the ones who felt that most powerfully.

WILLIAMS

Oh yes, we felt it much more strongly.

HENNESSY

You were flesh of the Labour movement's flesh, Shirley, really, weren't you?

WILLIAMS

That's right. And family of the family. Oh, absolutely. And I think both David and Roy, for other reasons, had shifted away from it some years earlier. I mean still quite a lot of me is still a social democrat, I can't deny it.

HENNESSY

I'd have thought every particle of you was, to be honest. [*Williams laughs*]

WILLIAMS

Yes, but there are things that my dear coalition does that I find quite hard to swallow down.

HENNESSY

We'll come back to that in a minute. But you make the break with the Gang of Four; the dear, sweet Michael Foot, who you loved dearly, was leader by this stage and begged you to stay, but you couldn't – you had to go in the end, didn't you …

WILLIAMS

Michael was a wonderful advocate and a wonderful writer; I don't think he was actually a natural political leader. He was a lovely man, no doubt. But as a political leader he probably didn't have the capacity for coming to terms with power in the way that, for example, Jim and also Harold had. So I don't think he would have ever actually managed to pull Labour out of this terrifying downward spiral it was going through. No, we had made our mind up by that time, so we had to stick with it. Though I should add to that, as you probably know Peter, that our last hope was Denis Healey – so many people's last hope. If he had won the election for leader, I think I would certainly have stayed for a bit longer, and then tried to back him and turn the Labour party back to what I regarded as its major job.

HENNESSY

You gave up in effect – when you went off with the so-called Gang of Four – your chance of becoming a Prime Minister, Shirley, because you were talked of as a Prime Minister. For a while, you were ahead of Mrs Thatcher in people's betting on who would be the first woman prime minister in the UK.

WILLIAMS

[*Laughing*] Well, two things. First one, you're quite right: I did give it up, and I realised that it would never happen. But also, I never had the simple targeting of purpose that she had. That's very important. She knew exactly what she wanted to be, and what she wanted to do, and she stood on a lot of people on her way. I think I was always more comfortable as a member of a team than as the single leader, whereas in her case she was much more happy being the single leader than being a member of the team. So it's partly psychological. I don't blame anybody for my not being prime minister except myself.

HENNESSY

You said of Michael Foot that he didn't have the necessary brutality to be prime minister.

WILLIAMS

Yes.

HENNESSY

Just simply not tough enough. Do you think that applies to you as well?

WILLIAMS

Probably.

HENNESSY

So no regrets?

WILLIAMS

[*Pause*] No –

HENNESSY

Not making it to Number 10?

WILLIAMS

No, no regrets.

HENNESSY

There's a conventional wisdom about the impact of the SDP-Alli-
ance, what became the Liberal Democrats, through the various
mutations. One is, that by splitting the centre-left vote, you handed
the bulk of the '80s to the Conservative Party, and indeed the early
'90s. And the other is that you paved the way for Tony Blair, you
so shocked the Labour Party that it was forced to modernise. That
you were a catalyst, though you never actually got the commanding height, or even got anywhere near sharing the commanding
heights with the two big parties. Now those are the conventional
wisdoms, as you know, about the impact of what you and Bill
Rodgers and David Owen and Roy Jenkins and the others did.
Now what's your reading of all that?

WILLIAMS

OK, the second one is quite right, your second proposition which
is that we, unknowingly, if you like paved the way for Tony Blair.
That's true. The Labour party got in total despair about its inabil-
ity, after three elections, all lost, to get back to government again.
They were prepared to swallow down – in a way, I never thought
they would – a wine bottle with a quite different wine inside it. It
still had the name, 'the Labour party', but it was a totally different
kind of Labour Party. It wasn't even social democrat, it was sort
of half way to being Christian Democratic, it wasn't a party of the
far left of centre or even the middle left of centre; it was the centre,
really.

I think in the case of the first proposition, it's not true. If you
look at the way in which voting broke down, a substantial number
of people in the income groups that normally vote Conservative
– a substantial number, not a majority, but a substantial minority
– moved away from the Conservative party, partly because these

were people who were anti-Thatcherite. They tended therefore to move to the SDP, because the idea of going to what was a very left-wing Labour party was unthinkable to them. So I reject that one. The second one I think is fair, and people like me have to live with that consequence – which wasn't all bad in some ways.

HENNESSY

Why didn't you rejoin the Labour Party?

WILLIAMS

Oh, really, I mean partly because ... [*laughing*]. First of all, I didn't think it was a social democratic party, in a funny way. Let me take one example, there's no time for many. It had a very bad record on civil liberties, in my view; it was over-run by the Home Office; it was not particularly good on prisons, and I had been a prison minister for a while; it was not very good on civil liberties – it was quite good on race, but it wasn't good on the basic freedoms that I believe are part of what the social democrats were all about. So that was a very central reason why I didn't rejoin it.

HENNESSY

Coming to the coalition, where we now are. Watching you in the House of Lords, as I do quite a bit, because I sit opposite you pretty well, it seemed to me, on the Health and Social Care bill that it was a real strain for you, because you're a child of 1945, believe in the '48 version of it, free at the point of delivery, which we all sign up to, but in that Health and Social Care bill – which you spent hours on, Shirley –

WILLIAMS

Hours.

HENNESSY

It seemed to me that the two great weather systems of post-war British politics were fighting it out in every other clause: there's the

Clem Attlee, Nye Bevan, free at the point of delivery, we're all in it together, social solidarity for ever, all that; and the more market impulses of Mrs Thatcher's era. And it was a terrible strain for you, Shirley, because you had to try and be loyal to the coalition, and yet we all knew your heart wasn't in it.

WILLIAMS

Well I think I sounded quite as if my whole heart wasn't much in it. Behind the scenes, I was pushing as hard as I could. And we did come out against some of the obvious things. For example, the most key thing, I think, which nobody ever notices was that we managed to get the Secretary of State for Health back into the position of being responsible, albeit at one remove, for the health service. What that meant was, to put it very crudely, that the NHS survived.

Under the previous Secretary of State for Health, Andrew Lansley, you remember that the bill as it started said in very clear terms that the Secretary of State for Health would no longer have any direct responsibility for any part of the NHS; it would all be the responsibility of GPs, now turned into so-called CCGs[1]. That was the crucial constitutional change. And by getting Margaret Jay and, possibly even more importantly, the great Lord Mackay of Clashfern on board to say that this was not constitutionally acceptable that such huge sums of public money should have no minister who is ultimately responsible for the way it was spent and what it was spent on, by doing that I think we did take a key step towards what I've always believed in with the NHS – that you have to build up, in the end, a cross-party consensus behind it. I don't think it can survive if it's tossed to and fro between parties, and between private and public, so that there's never any time for the poor thing to settle down and stop being endlessly reorganised. I don't know how far we achieved that – there's some hope we may.

---

1 Clinical Commissioning Groups

But I'm proud that it's still something called the NHS; it still is the major supplier of health in this country. And we did take very strong views on such things as, for example, the role of competition policy, the responsibility of Monitor to ensure that patients' interests came before competition, and various other things of that kind. And a lot of that was behind the scenes, not noticed by some of the big pressure groups of the country, who got across the idea that the Liberal Democrats were somehow very keen on privatising the health service. That was never true. We had managed, in my view, to save the NHS – though it's not quite exactly as I would like it to be.

HENNESSY

Shirley, you've always had a twin-track life, in the sense that you were a natural academic, and always interested in the political-science literature, as well as actually doing the political science life. And through that, you met your second husband, Dick Neustadt, the great Harvard figure, the greatest scholar of US presidency. He must have made a great difference to you.

WILLIAMS

Yes, he did, but not in the ways you'd expect. Not by being a grand man. But because he'd already achieved so much he didn't have any resentment at all about what I did. He found it amusing, and entertaining, and challenging, and exciting. He was also a wonderful man to be married to, because his previous wife, who was a great friend of mine, died of multiple sclerosis some years of course before we got married – and in that I began to see in him his total belief in the idea of marriage, which goes through every weather, every climate, but you're still there – I mean, it's Shakespeare, really. And that was wonderful because I always knew I could rely on him, not to praise me, but to tell me exactly the way things were as he saw them, but to do that with such love that you had to accept that they were almost certainly not only well-intentioned but true.

HENNESSY

Shirley, what kind of trace do you think you'll leave on history?

WILLIAMS

[*Pause*] Not a lot.

HENNESSY

Are you sure?

WILLIAMS

Well, I'll tell you where I will leave a trace – I find myself more of a model of what women can be than perhaps would have been the case before I started battling on these things. I'm a bit of a model to young people, and I have quite an influence – which will not last, it never does – through television and broadcasting, and that's essentially a rather short-lived thing. I hope that at the end of the day, some of the things that I have stood for – Europe, comprehensive schools etc – will survive and last in some form. But I have to say, quite honestly, that the area where I would have loved to have had some impact, but haven't, is on the nature of companies and the involvement of people in them. We haven't got away in Britain from the sharp divisions between shareholders, managers, workers. We haven't completely destroyed the class system, though I think we've gone some way towards it. The area where we have done well I think, and I really applaud this, is we are generally a multicultural and multiracial society, not totally but we've gone a long way in that direction. And that's something I'm very pleased about.

HENNESSY

Regrets?

WILLIAMS

Not really.

HENNESSY

You don't do regrets, Shirley.

WILLIAMS

[*Laughing*] Don't do regrets! Do tiredness, but don't do regrets.

HENNESSY

Shirley Williams, thank you very much.

WILLIAMS

Thank you.

Jack Straw

Series 1, Episode 2, first broadcast 18 July 2013

Born 3 August 1946. **Educated** Brentwood School; University
of Leeds; President, National Union of Students, 1969–71

MP (Labour) Blackburn 1979–2015

Home Secretary, 1997–2001; Foreign and Commonwealth Secretary,
2001–06; Lord Privy Seal and Leader of the House of Commons,
2006–07; Lord Chancellor and Secretary of State for Justice, 2007–10

Autobiography *Last Man Standing*, 2012

HENNESSY

With me today is a classic 'man of government', a politician far
more at home in Whitehall than opposing from Westminster. The
title of his autobiography, *Last Man Standing*, makes a virtue of
him being the great survivor of the Blair and Brown Cabinets.
He is also, by his own admission, a man who could – had he so
chosen – have kept Britain out of a scarring and controversial war
in Iraq. Jack Straw, welcome. Jack, it's a long way from a council
house on the north-east rim of London to the marbled floors of
the Foreign Office. You really are the incarnation of the post-war
baby boomer: August '46 you came into this world, 12 months after
the end of the war. You're one of Attlee's children, and I think you
carry that with you, right through.

STRAW

Yes, I think I do. My mother recently died, and in her papers I found this extraordinary letter that she had written to the *News Chronicle* – then a major newspaper on the left – just after the war, in which she had pleaded for German prisoners of war to be sent home to their families, rather than just punished further for having lost the war. And with that letter was a letter from the editor of the *News Chronicle*, written in hand, thanking her for this. Scores of letters had been sent to her about how sensible she had been. And what came through this was the extraordinary optimism of the Attlee period, and the sense that people like my mother – who was a teacher, but who came from a completely working-class background – their sense that at last, they owned the future. And that was a very powerful force that was conveyed to my siblings and to me, throughout our childhood.

HENNESSY

Your political formation … I think you were quite precocious really because I think you started keeping a personal archive of notes and papers when you were a teenager, just a teenager at school. Does this suggest you had a cunning plan of a nice pathway eventually to the Premiership, or were you just a precocious, unusually self-aware youth?

STRAW

I started earlier than that, actually, because I started when I was about nine. The only thing really that my parents agreed about was their politics and at that stage their pacifism. My father had been a pacifist during the war. And so we were members of the Peace Pledge Union. And my sister and I wrote to the man running the Peace Pledge Union, and we were then put on the subscription list for *War Resisters' International*, and so I kept all of those, and the correspondence. I was just a squirrel. But also, because of the breakdown of my parents' marriage, I think I became quite a solitary child as well. So retreating into records and newspaper cuttings and a life outside was a way of defending myself against what was a pretty bloody awful situation going on downstairs in the kitchen.

HENNESSY

Was there a spark of political ambition though as well? You knew you were a man of the left.

STRAW

No, it was when I went away to school – went to Brentwood – and found myself as somebody from very different circumstances from most of my peers in the boarding house, and needed to survive, and I became a kind of house socialist. I liked argument, which was just as well; it was one way of surviving in a very difficult environment. And in September 1959 a general election had been called by Harold Macmillan. I'd been sent out dishing out leaflets round the council estate we lived on, for the hapless Labour candidate for Chigwell and Ongar division. I read one of these leaflets of our candidate and thought it sounded a much better idea to become a member of Parliament for the Labour Party, far more productive, than dishing out leaflets on wet Wednesday afternoons. And then the local Labour Party decided on what I later learned was a gimmick, which was to have me make the opening speech at the formal adoption meeting for the Labour candidate. The speech went down rather well, and the local paper wanted a photograph of me, and the only photograph we had was of me wearing my school boater. So there is this young socialist, standing in his granny's back garden, wearing a boater. I think the paradox of this might not have been lost on the readers of the *West Essex Gazette*.

HENNESSY

A singular beginning of a political career. It was a tough time you had at home, your parents not getting on, and there was the unbelievable trauma of your father having tried to gas himself. I mean, utterly searing, Jack.

STRAW

Well, it's extraordinary what children put up with, and plenty of other children in that period, and today in other countries, put up with much worse. But it was awful. Because on the Friday I had happened to see two of my uncles put my father against the wall of my grandmother's house and knock his teeth out. This was because he'd been unpleasant, as he had been, to my mother. And then the next day we were playing outside and I went into the kitchen of our maisonette, up the stairs, smelled gas and found my father making what was rather a half-hearted attempt to gas himself, although he could easily have blown up the whole house. And then hearing my mother get very impatient with him; she said to him, 'If you want to kill yourself, that's all right, but please don't do it in front of the children'. So there was a kind of brutality in their relationship.

HENNESSY

Your mother was a remarkable woman.

STRAW

She was, she was.

HENNESSY

Formidable in every way. I never met her, but she had a great reputation, Jack, and obviously you carry the particles of your mother's formation with you.

STRAW

She was the most important influence on me by a long way. She'd had to put up with very great adversity. She was a sort of classic Attlee socialist, because she had a very strong belief in helping people who needed help, but she had very, very powerful social aspirations for herself, and she wanted to break out of the working-class, lower-middle-class environment in which she'd been brought up, and become more middle-class, and saw nothing wrong with that, no contradiction between that and her values. So she was very taken with people who were sort of socialist toffs, a lot of people involved in an organisation called Forest School Camps, who lived in Hampstead and Highgate. That kind of group, the people who were around AS Neill in the progressive-school movement. A really, really interesting woman with a passion for nursery education, which was there the whole of her life; she became a headteacher in the dockland area of Newham for quite a long time, and did great work for children there. But she pushed her kids. And I wanted to go to boarding school anyway – it seemed like a good way of getting away from the rumpus of what was going on. But she essentially got her satisfaction through the achievements of her children.

HENNESSY

Do you think, Jack, there may be a pattern in your life? You've always relied on the kindness of strong ladies: Barbara Castle, your great friend and patron, and Alice, your wife. Do you think that Joan implanted that in you, because she was the rock of the family?

STRAW

I've never thought of that before, but I think there's a lot in that; the patronage of strong ladies. I like to think my relationship with my wife is more than about patronage, but anyway! [Laughs] She's certainly robust in coming forward with advice.

HENNESSY

One of the most surprising and also candid sections in your memoir is about what you call the 'impostor syndrome' that's broken out throughout bits of your life, that feeling that 'Surely I'm going to be exposed', and all the rest of it. Now that's very surprising, Jack, for those who only know you from the external Jack, holding all these great offices of state, a presence in political life for an extraordinarily long time. But where do you think that comes from? Do you think it comes from the uncertainty of that fragile childhood?

STRAW

Oh, I'm not in any doubt it comes from that. And the sense that if you came from that kind of background, you didn't really deserve the success that you were achieving. The old sort of Groucho Marx observation, 'How could I become a member of a club that was willing to take me as a member of the club?'

HENNESSY

Do you still feel that, at times?

STRAW

No, I don't. I've got over that: years of therapy and a recognition that actually my career wasn't too bad at all. No, I don't feel that, but it was a very powerful sense for me, particularly through the '70s and '80s. I'd had a great time at university, I'd become President of the National Union of Students; I didn't have the impostor syndrome there at all, I was absolutely on top of the job. I did my bar finals very well, got a pupillage. But then all sorts of set-backs took place, not least in my private life, because of the difficulty in my relationship with my first wife: she got anorexia, she then got pregnant, and then we had this very wanted child, who was declared fit and healthy, and then died six days later. And that was awful. And then I get the nomination for Blackburn, it's a safe seat, I think, thank God for that; I get elected, pretty straight-forwardly; and then 18 months later, the Labour Party starts to fall apart.

HENNESSY

This is '79 and the aftermath of Labour's defeat.

STRAW

Yes, the aftermath of Labour's defeat. Benn and Co were trying to wreck the party, as it were, from the left; you had the Social Democratic Party, the people on the right of the party, trying to destroy the party from that wing. And it was a nightmare, literally a nightmare. Terrible. And then suddenly the Boundary Commission announced that 20,000 new voters are being added to my seat, and all the predictions are I'm going to lose. And on top of all of that the thing that triggered me to go and have psychoanalysis, was that one weekend I started to feel funny noises in my right ear, and over the space of the weekend I'd lost my hearing entirely in my right ear. It had been replaced with tinnitus, and there was a danger I'd lose it in my left ear. So if you add all that up together, I ended up really severely depressed. That's why my mother-in-law did me a great favour by recommending I see a psychoanalyst, which I did very intensively for about eight years.

HENNESSY

And it worked, Jack.

STRAW

And it worked, yeah. And I thought, well, you know, this is part of my story, I need to share this with people, so that I show to people that you can succeed while having this kind of background and while having these kind of monsters and impostors in your head. And the way I put it is this: these days, everybody accepts that you need to keep yourself physically fit, and there will be a period in your life when that fitness in challenged in one way or another, and you do something about it. You may break your leg, you may have an internal operation, well fine, you can get over it, and you can talk about it perfectly naturally. I think we're moving to a situation where we can talk about keeping ourselves psycho-logically fit. And our psychological state is partly dependent on us, but it's also dependent on where we've come from and on our childhood. So let's be open about this. It's been really interesting, the letters I've received. I had one the other day, actually from somebody who'd worked for me in the Civil Service, who said that reading my book had led her to seek help for her severe depression. And I said to my wife, I said to Alice, 'It was worth writing the book, just to save that one soul.'

HENNESSY

We've mentioned Barbara Castle; she was the most remarkable woman. I'm sure she's still remembered, in our generation she most certainly is, but I'm not sure if the flavour, the very distinc-tive flavour of Barbara has carried through to the younger genera-tions. Encapsulate her for me.

STRAW

Barbara Castle was the Labour Party's Margaret Thatcher. They were two peas in the same pod; quite remarkable similarities. And had Barbara not screwed up *before* a leadership election, rather than in Mrs Thatcher's case, 10 or 11 years after she'd become Prime Minister, Barbara could easily have been Labour leader, and probably Labour Prime Minister.

HENNESSY

And she screwed up over 'In Place of Strife', which tried to curb trade-union power in the late '60s.

STRAW

Yes, she screwed up over 'In Place of Strife', the right policy, but she pursued it in entirely the wrong way. So the Cabinet found out about this policy, which she and Harold Wilson had cooked up, from the pages of the *Financial Times*, and this apparent ambush by Barbara and Harold Wilson led to retaliation by Jim Callaghan – Callaghan, the Home Secretary, used his membership of the National Executive Committee to move a resolution to over-rule the Cabinet. Absolutely extraordinary. But Callaghan succeeded, and she was wounded, and she was only going to be there, after that, as long as Harold Wilson was there. Like Margaret Thatcher, she had an extraordinary sense of herself as a woman in a male world. She was contemptuous of women who wanted special treatment. She was very feminine, but she knew how to operate in masculine ways. She was totally competitive with her peers, again, as Margaret Thatcher was, and contemptuous of them. She was a nightmare to work with, but she was brilliant to work for.

HENNESSY

She brought you in as her special adviser, in '74, when Labour returned to power, because, she said later, of your guile and low cunning. Is that a compliment entirely, Jack?

STRAW

It was meant as a compliment – but I also think it was accurate. What happened was this: Barbara Castle had to see some senior visiting foreign dignitary. I think to help the meeting, both her special advisers were invited as well: one was Professor Brian Abel-Smith, professor of Social Administration at the LSE, very distinguished individual, and the other was me, J. Straw, aged 28. And the visiting dignitary asked Barbara what we two did, so quick as a flash, she said that she'd hired Brian for his brains, and J. Straw for guile and low cunning. And it sort of stuck, and I've used it against myself ever since. It says something, I suppose, about what I have to offer, though I'd like to think I have other things to offer as well.

HENNESSY

After Jim Callaghan becomes Prime Minister and sacks Barbara Castle – to her fury – you worked for Peter Shore. Very different man. Very interesting man. Again, not remembered to the degree that he should be, I think. What did you learn from Peter Shore?

STRAW

Peter Shore shared with Barbara the most important thing you need in politics, which is a strong sense of conviction. What you're doing with your life, what you believe in. Beyond that, they were very different characters. He was much more cerebral, much more the gentleman. Where Barbara often over-reached herself, Peter often held back too much. He could have become leader of the party had Michael Foot not intervened disastrously and at the last minute when candidates were lining up to succeed Jim Callaghan. And I was with Peter on a Friday when Michael Foot came into Peter's room and said, 'On Monday, I, Michael Foot, will announce my backing for you, Peter Shore, to be leader of the Labour party,' and I was also there on the Monday, when Michael Foot came in, scratched everything there was to scratch on his person, shifted from foot to foot, as well he might, and said to Peter, 'As you know, I did say I was making a statement about the leadership today, and that's true, but the statement is going to be that I'm going to be the leader, and I'm standing for leadership.' Peter, to his great credit, asked all his supporters, including me, to vote for Michael if he, Peter, lost the first ballot, which he was bound to. So we did. I also have to say that at that stage, Michael Foot and Denis Healey were much more evenly balanced. Denis had made himself so unpopular in so many ways that it was quite easy to vote for Michael with a clear conscience.

HENNESSY

Is your conscience clear now? This is 1980, and the Labour Party is really going into a civil war, which you hated every minute of. That you, Jack Straw, man of government, by voting for Michael seriously increased the chance of you, Jack Straw, never having a chance to be a minister, of any kind – it was very odd, paradoxically, looking back, that you should do that.

STRAW

It was a bad decision. In a way, although one shouldn't push the parallel too far, it was a bit like actively supporting Gordon Brown in 2007. The problem is, you can only measure people's propensity for a future job on the way they've performed their jobs up to then.

HENNESSY

But – I don't want to rub it in, Jack – but you compounded in the early '80s this strange misjudgement of yours, as I would see it, by voting for Tony Benn for the deputy leadership, and not for Denis Healey.

STRAW

Well look, the two are different. My vote for Michael Foot was rational at the time; my vote for Tony Benn was really out of cowardice, and I was ashamed of it. I still am. But my world was falling apart. I was under huge pressure in Blackburn, they were trying to deselect me ...

HENNESSY

This Militant Tendency stuff ...

STRAW

Militant Tendency, and others. And Benn was ruthless. Underneath this upper-middle-class veneer – utterly ruthless in pursuit of his own ambition. So we had people in the constituency party who weren't in Militant interestingly but in the softer end of the hard left, who were intimidating me and saying I'd lose my seat and all the rest of it. And in the end I'd convinced myself that the best thing to do was to get this damn man Benn elected as deputy leader and let him see what he could do with it, with his position.

HENNESSY

Looking back, aren't you relieved that Labour lost the 1983 election in a way, because if that manifesto had been carried through, famously the longest suicide note in political history as Gerald Kaufman called it, we might well have come out of Europe, and we would have given up the nuclear weapon, or Michael would have tried to; and in many ways some would argue that would have made you, a) unelectable ever again, at least for the foreseeable future, and, b) given the SDP the propellant it needed to become the party of the centre-left.

STRAW

We were never going to win the '83 election. But the issue in the '83 election was whether we stayed in business. And we only just beat the share of the vote of the SDP-Liberal Alliance by one percentage point. We got many more seats than them, because of the first-past-the-post system, but it was a damn close-run thing. And it then took another nine years before the Labour Party ridded itself of this poison, this apostasy that had taken it over.

HENNESSY

Can we linger on the nuclear question for a minute? Because you came from a Peace Pledge Union home, you were campaigning for nuclear disarmament until, I think, a Communist member of CND said, 'The Russians must have their bomb because it's the Workers' Bomb, everybody else must give up theirs' [*laughing*], and that's when I think scales fell from your eyes ...

STRAW

They did. I still remember. I think we were marching on the Aldermaston march between Reading and Slough. Drizzle. There'd been the usual songs which kept us going, 'Down by the Riverside' and all those other things, and then I got talking to this guy from Loughton CND. What people forget these days is that CND was completely penetrated by the Communist Party. And I was saying – wide-eyed, aged 14 – that we needed unilaterally to disarm, because then the Americans would, and then the Soviet Union would.

HENNESSY

This is 1960. Height of the Cold War.

STRAW

Height of the Cold War. So this man said, 'Yes son, you're absolutely right about the United Kingdom abandoning its bomb, and you're right about the United States' – as it were the great Satan – 'but you're wrong about the Soviet Union.' So I said, 'Why?' And he said, 'Well, it's a Workers' Bomb.' So we had a brief conversation about the Workers' Bomb. And then I could almost feel the scales falling from my eyes, and I'm thinking, hang on, this is a load of nonsense. So it led to the beginnings of a high level of scepticism about CND.

HENNESSY

It's a long trail from that Aldermaston march to you being Foreign Secretary, and being one of Tony Blair's alternative nuclear decision takers. If he'd been wiped out by a pre-emptive nuclear strike, and you'd been in a protected place and survived, it would have fallen to you to decide whether one of our Royal Navy missiles – Polaris or Trident in those days – would have been launched against the person who'd attacked the UK. Now that's a most extraordinary transformation. I think you're the only ex-CND person who's been in that position ... [*Straw laughs*]

STRAW

Well, I was CND as a teenager. You go through a transition in your life. I, fairly quickly, by my early 20s, had completely abandoned any idea of pacifism and unilateralism. But if you take these jobs, you've got to take the responsibilities that go with them; and one of the things I discovered about myself quite early on was that I was capable of responsibility, and capable of making decisions. Thinking about them very carefully, making the decisions, then getting on with the next one. Which is a fundamental characteristic that you need if you're going to be a minister. So of course I took those responsibilities very seriously, though it was slightly abstract because we were unlikely to launch a nuclear attack on anybody, or have one launched on us. The less than abstract responsibility was the responsibility for deciding whether to send fighter planes up to intercept a passenger plane that had been hijacked.

HENNESSY

A British 9/11 …

STRAW

A British 9/11. And I had lots and lots of training for this, and I carried on that responsibility right until the end of the government in 2010. There was one terrifying Boxing Day when we were having lunch with friends in the Cotswolds, as we usually do on Boxing Day, and Downing Street got hold of me. I was put through to the control and told that they couldn't find the Prime Minister, but they'd got this aeroplane, a passenger plane, coming in to land. They'd lost all contact with it, and did we scramble the planes? So for about 20 minutes, I was the man who was having to decide whether to send the fighters up, and I got them ready, then Tony took over and by that stage, after a lot of signals to this aeroplane, the pilots had woken up out of their stupor and got back in contact with the control tower. But we could have taken that plane down.

HENNESSY

A very stretching 20 minutes.

STRAW

Oh, I can still remember every second of it.

HENNESSY

If the amazingly remote but absolutely cataclysmic contingency of a nuclear attack on this country had occurred, and it fell to you to decide, what would you have decided, Jack?

STRAW

It would have depended on the circumstances, and whether I felt that by launching a nuclear attack on the other country that would have made this country more or less safe. That's the issue.

HENNESSY

So, in certain circumstances you might have authorised it.

STRAW

Yes. I mean, very reluctantly – but you can't possibly agree to take on that responsibility, and then at the last moment say, oh, by the way, I'm a closet pacifist.

HENNESSY

One of the questions that's come right through our lifetime – those of us who were born post-war – is immigration, and the attempts to integrate people from the Commonwealth into British society, and the problems that that has caused. And you as Home Secretary were at the epicentre when the dreadful case of Stephen Lawrence, the murder of Stephen Lawrence[1], erupted into our consciousness. And it's run on ever since, as a kind of talismanic touchstone question, the Lawrence affair. How significant do you think all that was, and when it first broke into your domain as Home Secretary did you quite realise that it was going to have this percussive effect?

---

1 The black teenager Stephen Lawrence was murdered in south-east London in 1993. Difficulties in convicting his killers led to a public inquiry, which in 1999 concluded that the Metropolitan Police was 'institutionally racist'

STRAW

[*Pause*] I knew it was profoundly important, and I'd spotted that in opposition. It took me three months to get agreement about the terms of reference for the inquiry, but the Home Office and the Met were in for any inquiry provided it was not a forensic inquiry into the death of Stephen Lawrence and the failure of the murder investigation. So I knew that it was important. Frankly, I never anticipated that it would be as important, or as long-running. But one of the things that has driven my politics is a hatred of discrimination against people on the grounds of their colour, their religion, or indeed their sexuality. And I thought that, if I could do one thing as Home Secretary, it would be to get some sense of justice, not only for the Lawrence family but for people who are non-white, black or Asian. And one of the most remarkable things that happens to me is people coming up to me, still today, black or Asian people, and saying, 'Thank you'. And I sort of look at them, and think, what are they thanking me for? But they're thanking me for Lawrence.

HENNESSY

History will always linger on one particular patch of your career, which is as Foreign Secretary in the run-up to the Iraq war. And you've said publicly, you've written it too, that you could have stopped that, if you'd resigned – and I suspect even you alone, not relying on Robin Cook and Clare Short to be there buttressing it would have meant we wouldn't have taken part in that war. And I think, Jack, you're the only ex-British Foreign Secretary who can say that. It's the most extraordinary weight for anybody to carry, both at the time and subsequently; one of the things that will be with you till your last breath.

STRAW

Yes, it is a great burden. I felt it at the time, and it's not a conceit to say that I could have stopped it – it just happens to be true. I was well aware that if, in those closing days to the decision that was to be taken on the 18th of March, 2003, I had decided to resign then there would not have been a majority in the House of Commons; it's as straightforward as that. I tried to explain in my memoirs how I came to the alternative decision, and what drew me in to deciding, much later than Tony, that it was right to take military action against Saddam. But also to describe the dynamic that was taking place between myself and the French, and how angry I felt about the way that Chirac and de Villepin were operating, frustrated that they – if they'd made more sensible decisions – could in my judgement have joined with us, and we could have prevented a war, because we drew up these six benchmarks for Saddam that were going to be attached to the famous Second Resolution, and they were all benchmarks which were going to be achievable. The benchmarks were drafted by Hans Blix.

HENNESSY

The weapons inspector.

STRAW

The weapons inspector now running a mile from any responsibility, and pretending that his inspection reports had given Saddam a clean bill of health, which they certainly had not, quite the reverse. But the idea of the Second Resolution, as far as I was concerned, was to stop a war, not to start one. But I also became aware, in retrospect, of how you could be sucked into a decision-making process; and at each stage, the gate marked 'war' became wider and wider, and psychologically more enticing, whereas the one marked 'peace' became narrower and apparently more difficult. And it was that experience that significantly informed my judgement later that on no account were we going to get involved in military action against Iran, and that led to this rather unexpected alliance between Dominique de Villepin, the French Foreign Minister, Joschka Fischer, the German Foreign Minister, and myself, to negotiate with the Iranians, what became the E3 Formation.

HENNESSY

So you drew your own lessons from it all. But can we go back to those days before the invasion? The Butler Inquiry into Weapons of Mass Destruction in Iraq showed that the Attorney General's opinion was crucial to all this and the full Cabinet only saw what I would call the shrivelled version of it, at the last minute, on March 17. Now, you're a Cabinet government man, Jack, and it's quite wrong to reduce peace and war to process, but process is also crucial at such moments. Do you not think that that was an absolute failure of Cabinet government, that the full Cabinet neither asked for, nor was given, the very caveat-laden full Attorney General's opinion that you had seen earlier, and that you didn't actually bring it to the table yourself either in the Cabinet Room that day?

STRAW

I would not have run Cabinet in the way Tony did. And I share your view that process is profoundly important, because process gives you legitimacy. The difficulty about circulating the very lengthy opinion of the Attorney General was frankly that it would have been leaked, and it would have been selectively leaked. That was a problem by that stage.

HENNESSY

You're saying one of the Cabinet colleagues would have leaked it?

STRAW

Yes. If there had been a war cabinet, and if people had been taken into confidence at a much earlier stage, I think the psychology of the way the Cabinet was operating would have been very different, and that's how I would have handled it. And I don't think, then, that it would have leaked. But at that moment, given the way Tony had run his Cabinets for the previous six years, and was going to carry on, that was the difficulty. It also has to be said that the very long letter was Peter Goldsmith debating about the issues, saying

'On the one hand, and on the other', this, that and the other. The letter statement that he made on the 17th of March, the day before the vote in the Commons, was a letter of decision. So, having gone around the houses in early March and before that, he then came to a decision, and he himself has said that there was a very big distinction in terms of the quality of these documents, and what the Cabinet needed to know was, was he saying yes or no to whether it was lawful, not how did he arrive at that conclusion. By the way, even if all 20-plus pages of Peter's earlier *exegesis* had been circulated, there was nothing that the Cabinet could have done about it; this was a decision for the Attorney, and the Attorney alone.

HENNESSY

The great Lord Bingham, Senior Law Lord, argued later that legal opinions like that should be shared with Parliament and the public, on peace and war. If that had been shared with the public, the longer one, the House of Commons wouldn't have voted the way that it did, would it?

STRAW

I don't know, is the answer to that. I mean, Tom was a great jurist, but he had his political views about Iraq. And one of the truths about Iraq is that the lawyers involved made their decision on the lawfulness of Iraq by starting with their political and moral position on it. It's a universal truth: you won't find a single lawyer who was opposed politically to the war who said that the war was, nonetheless, lawful, and the reverse is also true. And that's the nature of international law. So, much though I loved Tom Bingham and revered him as a jurist, I don't place any greater credence on his opinions on that than any other lawyer's.

HENNESSY

One of the legacies, in your own mind, of this experience is your proposal for a Cabinet Government Act, to spell out what the

Prime Minister is for, and the relationship with the collective, and including the Chancellor of the Exchequer, which is a fascinating idea – and I should declare that you and I have talked about that, and we're going to do some work together on it. But in a way it's a most remarkably ripe, retrospective commentary on Tony Blair's style of leadership, and indeed, Gordon Brown's, which we'll come to in a minute.

STRAW

Yes. I owe Tony a huge amount; he essentially made my career after it was in the doldrums under John Smith. But I never approved of the way Tony ran government, and he knew that from a very early stage. [*Laughing*] There's a whole series of missives from me in the system, in which, from early on, I'm saying you need to make the process more formal, you need to involve your colleagues more. And that included a very long set of suggestions in 2003–2004 about how he should formalise the way government operated. He, in retrospect, was never going to do that because it wasn't his style and it wasn't his personality. The irony is that had he done it, his legacy would have been a better one. He would have got the same decisions out of the system, but people would have respected the decisions more. People can accuse me of being bureaucratic. I don't think I am, but I certainly believe in process. One of the things I learned very early on as a bar student was that procedure is about the most important, not the least important, subjects in the legal system, because it's the means by which people can access power, access their rights. And we neglect it too much within the British governmental system. And that's why I think there ought to be a Cabinet Government Act, which lays down what are the responsibilities of the Prime Minister, what are the responsibilities of the Cabinet; which prescribes that there should be a National Security Council, a very welcome but non-statutory development by David Cameron, that there should be an Economic Council, which has to look at budget proposals and public-spending proposals, and that only after that's happened can they come to Parliament; that also lays down the process for both the Cabinet, as well as Parliament, to decide on war and peace. These are necessary parts of a constitutional apparatus, and they ought to be down in black-letter law.

HENNESSY

Gordon Brown – a very different style to Tony Blair's, but you didn't throb with admiration for Gordon's style as Prime Minister either did you? When did you realise that it wasn't going to work? Because there was that amazing first Cabinet meeting, which went on for ever, looking at this draft Great Constitutional Reform Bill that was going to come forward. Did you realise that day, even though you'd been his campaign manager, that Jack was making the wrong decision again about people that had come to the fore?

STRAW

Well, it was a sort of an inevitable decision to have Gordon crowned as Prime Minister, because he was the only candidate. And people say, why didn't so-and-so stand, why didn't I stand? Well he had got the numbers lined up ... what would have been the point of standing when you were just going to get crushed? I was very taken with his constitutional proposals, and it fell to me, as kind of the point man, to implement them. I've got an abiding interest in the British constitution, and in the importance of change. I got a flavour for the chaotic way in which he made decisions in the drafting of what became the Governance of Britain proposals ...

HENNESSY

So very early on you realised that this man, for all his remarkable gifts, was not going to be able to hack it. He couldn't decide ...

STRAW

I mean, he did decide – even though bits were coming off the machine as he was deciding. But what traumatised the Cabinet, and led to this loss of confidence in him by his Cabinet colleagues, and in himself, was this paralysis of decision-making that took place at the Bournemouth Labour Party conference that took place in the early autumn of 2007, when he just allowed speculation about whether they should or should not call an election to take over the conference. He failed to quell that in his speech on the Tuesday, allowed that to go on right through to the following weekend into the Conservative Party conference, went off to Afghanistan in a flat-footed, ridiculous attempt to draw attention away from the Conservatives, misusing the power of the Prime Minister. And only at the end of that week, after the Conservatives had a field day with us, did he then say, 'Oh no, I've no intention of calling an election, and I don't know what all this speculation is about'. So it showed both that he was paralysed in terms of decision-making, but also had this remarkable propensity for double-think and disingenuity, which I'd not really understood was a characteristic of his until then.

HENNESSY

There's a very delicate question from your time as Foreign Secretary, when you authorised Secret Intelligence Service operations of the so-called rendition of the Libyan Islamist dissident, Abdel Hakim Belhadj. And I know there are legal processes going on, so you're probably mightily constrained about what you can say. But Foreign Secretaries do that; the SIS doesn't do special operations without the say-so of the Foreign Secretary.

STRAW

Well, let me say two things. One is, that in general I was assiduous in applying my legal responsibilities and duties to everything I did in supervising the Secret Intelligence Service, and indeed GCHQ.

The second thing is on this specific action – there is a legal action taking place at the moment, I'm a defendant in that, and I'm very sorry, but I can't say any more about that.

HENNESSY

If you had made it to the Premiership, what would it have been like? There's an inner safe, Jack, I suspect, at the back of your mind, in which the draft Queen's Speech for the first Straw Premiership is, somewhere. What would you have wanted to do, and how would you have set about it?

STRAW

I think I would have done OK. I think I would have surprised people. I would have formalised government, and I would have done a lot to hand back power to the House of Commons. My view is that the Whips' Office has over the years become far too powerful, that the crucial role of this place is legislation. And this place needs to have more power over it. So it would be all about that, making this place, the House of Commons, much more the cockpit of politics, than it is.

HENNESSY

Would you have removed the timetable from all government business, played with the so-called guillotining? Because it was the Blair government that did that ...

STRAW

This was so-called modernisation, which is not modernisation at all in my view. Some timetabling is sensible, and a fact of life these days, with more women MPs and more male MPs with young families, is that they want to have greater certainty about when they go home. But you could have a degree of timetabling without putting the House of Commons programme in a straitjacket.

HENNESSY

Jack, what trace do you think you'd like to leave on history?

STRAW

First, as someone who held very high office, but who carried on meeting his first duty, which is to represent his constituents. Secondly, to have made this place a fairer place, which is what I saw as my aim when I was Home Secretary, both making it safer …

HENNESSY

This place being the country …

STRAW

Yes, this place, the country. Making it safer, but also giving people more rights through measures like the Human Rights Act. And as Foreign Secretary, my responsibility for Iraq is indelible, it will always be there. But hopefully people will also recognise the work I did in trying to bring Turkey into the European Union, and above all, in stopping there being military action against Iran. And as I used to say to the Iranians, Joschka Fischer, Dominique de Villepin and I were their human shield, and they ought not to forget it.

HENNESSY

Jack Straw, thank you very much.

Norman Tebbit (Lord Tebbit)

Series 1, Episode 3, first broadcast 25 July 2013

Born 29 March 1931; **Education** Edmonton County Grammar School

MP (Conservative) Epping 1970–74; Chingford 1974–92

Parliamentary Secretary, Department of Trade, 1979–81;
Minister of State, Department of Industry, 1981; Secretary of
State for Employment, 1981–83; Secretary of State for Trade
and Industry, 1983–85; Chancellor of the Duchy of Lancaster,
1985–87; Chairman of the Conservative Party, 1985–87

Autobiography *Upwardly Mobile*, 1988

HENNESSY

With me today is one of the most flavourful and recognisable politicians of recent times. As long as the governments of Margaret Thatcher are remembered, he will be remembered too. In fact, if any single figure apart from Lady Thatcher herself could be said to be the incarnation of Thatcherism, it's Norman Tebbit. Norman, welcome.

TEBBIT

Thank you.

HENNESSY

Napoleon once said, if you want to understand a man or a woman, you need to think about the world when they were 20. You were 20 in 1951 – height of the Cold War, still the shadow of the Second World War rationing. What were the forces which contributed to your formation, as a human being and as a politician later?

TEBBIT

I've always maintained that if you grew up as I did, in the tail-end of the depression and high unemployment, in a family on the wrong side of the tracks so to speak, and then gone through the war, been bombed and evacuated and all that sort of thing, and then come out through all that into a post-war era where for years after the war we still rationed sweets even – you have to have concluded by then that there really ought to be a better way of running things than that. And I'd come to that conclusion by the time I was about 14 or 15, that there really ought to be a better way of running these things.

HENNESSY

Just by the end of the war, in fact.

TEBBIT

Yes, indeed. And by the time I was 15, I'd joined the Young Conservatives, determined that I was going to change the world. I suppose to some extent I chipped away at a few of the edges. [*Laughs*] But I was determined to make things different.

HENNESSY

Now many people listening would think that a young man, aged 15, from your background, tail-end of the slump, the shared privations of the war, would be tilted to the left by that experience. That things would be better, but only because the state continued to organise things to make them better, and the state had been remarkably well organised for the purposes of beating Hitler. So you were going against the tide even then.

TEBBIT

Yes – I think I have an anti-collectivist gene. That was essentially the thing: I was not a collectivist at any time in my life. And I saw all salvation as being a matter of what individuals could do, and that the function of the state was to enhance the ability and remove the barriers for the individuals to do that.

HENNESSY

Do you think you always liked going against the swim, the conventional wisdom?

TEBBIT

I don't know, perhaps I did at that time, but it just came naturally. It was the tide that flowed against me, not me against the tide!

HENNESSY

You said later in your autobiography that when you were in the Airline Pilots' Association it reflected your obsessive competitive qualities. You were very honest about that. Do you think, looking back, that Norman Tebbit the trade unionist was there in formation, up against the big battalions.

TEBBIT

Yes, I think so. Competitive. And it sounds odd to be a trade unionist when you're not a collectivist, but I'd got into the trades union primarily through its activities on the technical front. And the more I saw of the way that a nationalised industry was managed, the more I began to realise that I was rather sorry for the management, that it was impossible to manage it. But I had to fight my corner within that crazy world.

HENNESSY

Do you think the experience of being in the Royal Air Force Auxiliary added another layer of formation? Because it's the Cold War; if the Cold War had turned nasty in the early '50s, you'd have been in the front line, Norman, with that plane of yours.

TEBBIT

Indeed, we would have been in the front line. But I think also it brought me into touch with a different group in society. I was commissioned in the Royal Air Force, and I began to mix with men older than myself, much more experienced, war-time guys, professionals – my flight commander became my solicitor, the intelligence officer on the squadron was my bank manager, and so on. A different group of society. And I think that made quite a lot of difference to me; it made me a good deal more confident. If I'd been under-confident in the past, if you're wearing a uniform with a bit of braid on the cuff and a pair of Air Force wings on the lapel, you do have a little more confidence about meeting anyone else in life.

HENNESSY

Was that turn of the '50s your golden age? A society in many ways at ease with itself, for all its problems, for all the loss of wealth in the war, and all the class obsessions which were still everywhere. You do seem to me to be a man of the '40s and '50s. Do you think that's fair?

TEBBIT

I think there's something in that. Roy Jenkins famously said that the permissive society is the civilised society; I've taken the view over the years that the more permissive it has been, the less civilised it has been. I ask myself why it was possible for me, as a child, to walk home through the black-out, through totally darkened streets, safely – how many mothers would now let their child walk through the streets of Edmonton if all the lights were extinguished? Not many, I fancy. I liked that stability that there was in society; I liked the fact that people who didn't pay their bills at the grocer's were looked down on, and indeed snubbed. I felt there was a firmness in society at that time, of shared values. I have to confess that it may be that to some extent it's the working class adopting some of the nastier habits of the upper classes, as much as the other way around, that has caused society to deteriorate as much as it has.

HENNESSY

In the wider world in the '50s, 1953, Coronation year, the empire came home, the wonderful procession through the streets after the Coronation, troops from right across the globe and so on. Did it mean something to you? The extended Britain, as it were? Did you see it as an extended family, or great-powerdom – how did it work in the Tebbit mind?

TEBBIT

I think I did see it as a special place, which I later explored a good deal. I was conscious from very early days that English was the greatest language in the world; that we contributed a lot in terms of decent and reasonably corruption-free administration to the rest of the world; that whatever criticisms are made of our record in our colonial empire, I don't think there's any other European country that could point to a better record than ours, and there are sort of touchstones of that even now. I mean cricket is a game which is only played amongst the old imperial powers, and it's played in a great spirit of equality.

HENNESSY

You got into trouble on the cricket front later when you applied the cricket test – 'Which team do you support?' But if you take the extended family view of cricket it's all family, Norman, isn't it?

TEBBIT

Yes, there is a great deal of family. On a couple of occasions, I almost went to work out in the empire, I applied for a job in the Falklands – Lord knows what would have happened if I'd ...

HENNESSY

What job was that?

TEBBIT

Flying the ambulance float-plane round the islands. But since my flying at that time had been confined to fast jets I think they thought that probably I wasn't the right guy.

HENNESSY

'The Biggles years', if you'd done it ...

TEBBIT

I very nearly went off tea-planting in Assam. Very different careers that I might have followed! [*Laughing*]

HENNESSY

You're more of a romantic than people realise. [*Tebbit laughs*]

HENNESSY

The Conservative Party that you were active in in the late '40s, and ever since, really, was very big: it had one and half million members if not more in the early '50s; breathtaking to look back now, with Young Conservatives a great force in the land, and all that. But it wasn't the Conservative Party that was ideally constructed for a boy from Ponders End, was it?

TEBBIT

No, it wasn't; but then that's what making things happen is about, isn't it? You change things.

HENNESSY

Were you patronised by the others in the Conservative Party, as you rose through?

TEBBIT

I think if you ignore it, it goes away.

HENNESSY

You've always had reservations about the consensually minded Macmillan years, haven't you? I think you think quite a lot of rot set in, in one way or another, when Uncle Harold was in Number 10.

TEBBIT

I did indeed. I felt that the Conservative Party had lost its way quite badly in the early '60s, particularly under Macmillan. And I found his government was losing touch very badly in my view, and by that time of course I was married and had got a couple kids, and was busily earning my income, flying for BOAC. But I eventually got so cross about it that I put pen to paper and wrote to Iain Macleod, who was then chairman of the Conservative Party. And in it I set out what the government was doing wrong, and how it should be sorted out and what should be done; and Iain wrote back to me, and in essence said, 'Dear Norman, I understand you feel strongly about these things, and believe that you've got the answers to a lot of the problems. Why don't you come and help us?' And I read the letter several times, and then said to my wife, 'Damn it, I will.' I think that was in about 1964, somewhere like that.

HENNESSY

So Iain Macleod's letter was a trigger to tilt you from a Conservative party activist into actually pursuing a political career.

TEBBIT

That's right.

HENNESSY

It's a bit of a sacrifice, from being a BOAC pilot on the new and swanky Boeing 707, with a good income by the standards of those days, to the precariousness of being a candidate with a young family. Some say it's a chancer's profession, politics, because it's so unpredictable.

TEBBIT

It was a very chancy thing, because I stood in 1970 for the constituency of Epping, but because of the growth of Harlow New Town not least, it had double the appropriate electorate, about 120,000, so I knew it was going to be redistributed. I couldn't know what was going to happen; I wasn't even sure that I was going to win it in 1970, and it didn't quite accord with my game plan – I would have liked to have another five years building up my pension from BOAC! But I had to take a chance. You can't hesitate on these things. I took a pay cut of about 50% and a very insecure future.

HENNESSY

Did you think you had a star to steer by, to use a favourite phrase of Margaret Thatcher's? Are you a man of destiny on the quiet, Norman?

TEBBIT

I didn't think that I was destined to be even a minister, entering Parliament with no background at all in politics really, at the age of about 40. I was just content that I was going to go there and do something to make things different.

HENNESSY

Well, you certainly had an impact. People were extremely offensive to you, weren't they, within almost weeks. 'The half-trained polecat … the Chingford skinhead' – that was later on, admittedly. You've always been on the receiving end as well as giving it out, haven't you?

TEBBIT

Well, that's true and I was extraordinary grateful to Michael Foot for that comment about a semi-house-trained polecat, because it told me that I'd got under his skin, and it told the public at large that I was a chap Michael Foot had to take seriously. Nobody had heard of me; they'd all heard of Michael Foot. [*Laughing*] It was a fundamental error on his part.

HENNESSY

Did you begin to form a friendship, even an embryonic partnership, with Margaret Thatcher in your early years, even though she was bound by collective Cabinet responsibility. Did you see a kindred spirit there?

TEBBIT

I scarcely had any contact with her, really. A few words now and again, you know, when we met, perhaps in the library reading newspapers or something like that, and naturally being a small 'c' conservative, I had not considered the possibility of a woman leading the Conservative Party at that time.

HENNESSY

What did you make of her in those early conversations?

TEBBIT

Very impressive woman, you know. I realised quite rapidly that she and I thought along pretty closely similar lines about politics as a whole.

HENNESSY

Did you ever talk to her, in those days when you got to know her through the opposition years, when Labour was in office, '74-'79, about how both of you couldn't really abide the post-war consensus, felt smothered by it? Because she was always very eloquent about how much she loathed that post-war consensus, which pretty much everybody else in your generation had taken in with their mother's milk.

TEBBIT

Yes, I found that very refreshing, that I found somebody else who felt the same way about that post-war consensus. But also, of course, I think we both felt the same way about some of the things which that early Labour government, the '45 government, did, which were absolutely right, and which it would be have been much more difficult for a Conservative government to do at that time.

HENNESSY

Tell me. Such as?

TEBBIT

Membership of Nato. It was not Churchill that created Nato, it was Attlee.

HENNESSY

Ernie Bevin …

TEBBIT

Ernie Bevin in particular, one of the truly great men of British politics, in my judgement. And the British nuclear deterrent; again, how difficult would that have been if it had been a Conservative government trying to take that through against the Labour Party? And the Labour Party would have been against it.

HENNESSY

So you had conversations, you and Margaret Thatcher, about the Attlee government and the great things it did in that area?

TEBBIT

Oh, we did, as we got to know each other, it would come up – looking at those early post-war years, and what needed to be changed, and what was in fact a very good thing.

HENNESSY

And you would regard Clem Attlee and Ernie Bevin as 22-carat patriots, wouldn't you?

TEBBIT

There's no doubt whatsoever in my mind that in any really great *contretemps* that Attlee and Bevin and I would have been on the same side.

HENNESSY

In '79, you felt – you must have felt, given the financial position, the state of industrial relations – that there wasn't just one mountain to climb, there was a Himalayan range, really. And for all your combativeness, you must have felt daunted in May '79, when Mrs Thatcher came in with a 40-plus majority.

TEBBIT

It was clearly not going to be an easy time. What sticks in my mind about that era was that the TUC generals, not the shop floor workers but the TUC generals, had overthrown two governments running. Essentially they'd overthrown Ted Heath, and then they had overthrown Jim Callaghan. They were obviously spoiling for another fight, and seeking to overthrow Margaret Thatcher. That seemed to me something which could not possibly be allowed, so I knew it was going to be a struggle, that sooner or later they would attempt it, and I think Margaret did too.

HENNESSY

She first of all sent Jim Prior to Employment, who was a consensus man, and did make huge efforts to persuade the trade-union leaders that it couldn't go on like this. Do you think Jim failed, and if so why, and what lessons did you learn from Jim Prior as Employment Secretary when the job fell to you?

TEBBIT

My view was that it was inevitable that Jim was going to be Secretary of State for Employment – he'd been our spokesman. I think it would have been highly dangerous had we gone to the electorate saying, 'We're going to take on the unions; we're really going to sort 'em, to hell with what they think, we're going to do what we think', and all the rest of it; Jim's consensual approach was one which accorded with what most people probably thought. They thought there was a way through. Most people had bought into the idea that our industrial-relations problem was a load of Bolshy so-and-so's on the shop floor being restrained by these terribly responsible union leaders. I think that was the view that Jim had formed. My view was completely the opposite. I don't think many others held that view. [*Laughing*] And so everything I did was constructed around that belief, which I think has proved to be the correct one.

HENNESSY

The gods of politics were very kind to you, when you went to Employment, because as a young man on the *Financial Times,* you had been forced to join Natsopa, one of the print unions, if I remember, and suddenly, after all those decades had elapsed, there you were, in the driving seat, with the possibility of changing industrial-relations legislation – a belated justification for your loathing of what you'd been forced to do in the 1940s.

TEBBIT

Oh, I certainly bitterly opposed the closed shop in which I'd been involved by Natsopa, the union in those days. But there was another grudge, if that was a grudge, and that was that when my wife and I lived in London, we lived in the Barbican, and my wife had resumed her nursing career and was working at Barts Hospital. She became ill, but there was at the time a sort of Soviet that was seeking to run the hospital, and amongst the demands of the strikers involved at that time was that they were going to decide who could be admitted to the hospital on emergency grounds, and they decided, with all the wisdom of shop stewards, that my wife's case was not sufficiently urgent for her to be admitted to hospital. I think they realised afterwards that they must have made a mistake.

HENNESSY

Tell me about your first day in the Department of Employment, because Ernest Bevin, when he became minister of Labour and National Service, said to a journalist, 'Mr Gladstone, they say, was at the Treasury from 1868 to 1914. I'm going to be in the Ministry of Labour from 1940 to 1979' – metaphorically speaking. So you took over Ernie's legacy in many ways. But the officials probably didn't know what to make of you; they probably didn't know that you were a great fan of Ernest Bevin.

TEBBIT

No they didn't. Nor perhaps were they familiar with my theory of government, which is that all government departments exist to represent an interest in government; that's their being. The Department of Industry represents industrialists; the Department of Education represents educationalists, God forbid; the Foreign Office represents foreigners; and the Department of Employment thought they represented the TUC. I had to disabuse them of that. So the first thing I asked my permanent secretary was, 'What has happened to the bust of Ernie Bevin?', which I knew had always been on the ministerial floor just outside the lift. And he looked a bit embarrassed, and I said, well, where is it? 'Well, we moved it, we didn't think you'd want it.' I said, where is it? 'It's in the cellar.' So I said, 'Well send somebody down to bring it up and put it back where it should be, Ernie Bevin was the greatest minister of Labour that this country's ever seen.' So that was the first shock to them. [*Laughs*] And I continued with my shock treatment. I've always believed that you can get an idea through to somebody best when their defences are down; if they're laughing, they won't reject in a hostile manner. It'll go through, under their radar. So I got my officials around the table and told them that I was absolutely determined that I was going to change the whole of industrial-relations legislation in a way that it had never been changed before. I was going to repeal the 1906 Act, which is really like declaring yourself to be a republican while you're at church, or something.

HENNESSY

Protective picketing, and all that.

TEBBIT

Yes. So they began to blanch a bit, and I continued with my voice raising slightly. I said, 'Of course it will be difficult,' reminding them of the way that the Heath legislation had finished, with trade unionists who had got into jail and had to be released, to the humiliation of the government. I said, 'The Prime Minister knows what I'm going to do; if necessary we'll call the police; if necessary we'll call out the army; if necessary we'll build barbed wire barricades around every prison in the country, and we won't let any of those buggers fight their way in.' And at that stage they realised they were having their legs pulled. And they started laughing. And from there on I could not have had a better lot of guys working for me. I knew the basic philosophy and shape of the legislation I wanted, but it was they who turned it into legislation which has stood the test of time, in that it's not really been touched in the past 30-odd years.

HENNESSY

HENNESSY

It's interesting hear you say that, because in 2013 there's a lot of talk in the coalition government – indeed it's been made public by the minister for the Civil Service – about how many ministers are disappointed with their civil servants: 'They block, they won't listen, and we've got to give them commands and it doesn't happen', and there's a move to politicise the senior civil service, in some quarters. It's not put quite as directly as that, but that's what it means. How do you react to that?

TEBBIT

I think it would be a terribly great mistake. I don't want a politicised Civil Service. One should never forget that the Civil Service has to serve governments of all political persuasions. It must not be politicised in that sense. It would be a great mistake. I think too few ministers now spend enough time talking to their officials; they talk to their special advisers, who talk to their officials, and that's a fundamental error.

HENNESSY

It's one of the mysteries, I think, that future political historians might toy with about the Thatcher years in government, your years, is that you didn't seek to turn back some of those liberal or conscience reforms of the 1960s that you really didn't like. You had these big majorities, and yet you didn't reverse the legislation that you disliked so much, those social reforms of the '60s. Now why was that?

TEBBIT

I think one of the things I learned in government was that in a Cabinet of 20-odd people, it's unlikely that you're going to have more than half a dozen real drivers, a lot of competent people, yes, but people who really drive reform are in short supply. Parliament can only accept a certain amount of great reform at any time, and we had to concentrate on the most urgent issues: the trade-union problem was one of the great issues; the problem of the nationalised industries, which instead of creating wealth, actually consumed it; and the problem of the economy more broadly, the problems of inflation, and things of that kind. So we simply didn't have the manpower or the parliamentary time to conduct as many reforms as I would have liked. Indeed, probably the electorate would have said, no, no, that's too much. The electorate is 'small c' conservative in many ways as well; they don't want the whole world to be turned over at once.

HENNESSY

Would you like to have gone back on capital punishment, say, or homosexual rights for consenting adults, those kind of liberal reforms?

TEBBIT

I don't think that would have been sensible. I think there's a lot to be said for the concept of capital punishment, but I think that would have been, again, a step too far. I think there's a much greater tolerance of some behaviour which deviates from the norm, let me put it in that sense, and I think it will be difficult even if one wanted to, to reverse those reforms.

HENNESSY

One of your other regrets, looking back, I think, was that the pit closures were too rapid and too extensive. You've been very eloquent about the destruction of the pit communities, these fine working-class communities, and the problems it's brought. You feel that very deeply, don't you, and yet the orthodox view of you, Norman, is, 'Well, he's a hard man, that one – if anybody was going to take on the miners with Mrs T, it was him.' You do feel that , don't you – there is a scar there, a scar of regret.

TEBBIT

There is a scar of regret. But of course, it wasn't Mrs T that took on the miners, it was Arthur Scargill that took on Mrs T. And he couldn't carry all the miners with him. But I've always been conscious of the fact that the miners did form an elite within the working class, for want of a better expression, and a lot of what they were doing was *absolutely* that they were building their own little societies in which they behaved with enormous courage at times, and certainly with great integrity.

HENNESSY

The other event of the '80s that you'll always be remembered for is the ghastly tragedy of the Brighton bomb. It is impossible for somebody who hasn't experienced that to have any real idea of what people go through, particularly if a person you love dearly is seriously injured, and you were pretty badly injured too. I hope you don't think it's impertinent, but could you describe a bit how that changed you, that experience?

TEBBIT

I'm not sure that it changed me very much, and I don't like the idea that there was something unique about that experience. After all, an awful lot of people were buried alive in the ruins of bombed buildings between 1939 and 1945, and we're not expected to make an undue fuss about it, but to crawl out, or be dragged out, and get on. But it made a great deal of difference to me, of course, because I felt like I had to put my wife's interests ahead of my own, and I have never forgiven the Establishment, in its broadest sense, for the fact that although we've had enquiries into so-called Bloody Sunday, although we're now apologising for what we did to protect the Kikuyus against Mau Mau, whenever I gently suggest that it would be a good idea to have an enquiry to nail those who were really responsible for that terrorist atrocity, not the poor little creature that planted the bomb, but those who planned it, organised it, authorised it, financed it ...

HENNESSY

The army council of the IRA in other words ...

TEBBIT

Well, yes indeed, so I believe; they did after all claim credit for it, if credit be the right word. Whenever I suggest it would be a good idea to actually have an inquiry which named those people, so that we could all see them in their full glory, I'm told that that would be a very bad thing to do.

HENNESSY

Despite the strength of feeling that you've just expressed, Norman – do you not think it's remarkable that Northern Ireland has got to where it is now? If you'd been Prime Minister in the early '90s, and not John Major, and the message had come through the back-channel from the IRA that the war is over – would you have grabbed it?

TEBBIT

Let's be careful to get it right. What came from the IRA was the belief that they were on the rocks. The IRA had been infiltrated to a great extent; they were in deep trouble.

HENNESSY

British Intelligence had penetrated them?

TEBBIT

Indeed, British Intelligence had penetrated them. One of leading members of the IRA was about to be indicted, I believe, for no less than eight murders. He would probably have been found guilty. He would probably have gone to jail. I think the motivation was fear of what was happening to them. I like to think that had Airey Neave lived, that fear would have come much earlier.

HENNESSY

Mrs Thatcher's adviser on Northern Ireland, who the INLA[1] murdered.

TEBBIT

Indeed. Had Airey Neave not been murdered on the eve of the 1979 election, he would have become Secretary of State for Northern Ireland, and I think he would have approached the problem from a slightly different direction; and we would have got to at least where we are, perhaps a bit beyond, very much earlier.

HENNESSY

Of course, the other impact in terms of public and political life was that – because of the commitment you made to your wife, Margaret – Mrs Thatcher lost you as a ministerial colleague in '87, after the election. That must have been a very difficult decision for you, and indeed when Mrs Thatcher tried to get you back in again, you must have been really torn.

TEBBIT

Yes. I'd had to tell her, of course, that I would not be available to stay in the Cabinet after the '87 election. She found that difficult to accept; she even set Willie Whitelaw one me, [*laughing*] to try to persuade me, and as everyone knows Willie is a very persuasive man! But I had to stand by what I promised my wife. And then in 1990, when things were becoming very difficult for her, she asked me if I would go back into the Cabinet, and again I faced that

---

1 Irish National Liberation Army, a republican group

terrible conflict between divided loyalties. But my undertakings to my wife pre-dated, and they had to stand. And then in 1990, of course, when she was brought down, again, colleagues asked me if I would stand for the leadership; and it was a very, very difficult decision. Who knows, I might have been elected, I might not. I don't know. It wasn't easy.

HENNESSY

Do you think you could have saved Margaret Thatcher in November 1990, if you'd been in the Cabinet with her? I've never seen a more dramatic moment in the House of Lords since I've been in the chamber, than during the tributes to her in the spring of 2013, when you said, 'My great regret is that I left her to the mercy of her friends', and you looked down to the senior Conservative Cabinet ministers on the Privy Council bench, where I notice you never sit, and there they were. It was drama with a capital D that was Norman. But do you think, if you had been with her, you could have seen them off, in November 1990 – or had things got to such a pitch that even you, if you'd interposed your body, couldn't have done it?

TEBBIT

I think I could have held them back for a while. I don't think I could have seen them off. I've always taken the view that when somebody becomes Prime Minister and they walk through that door and look out of the windows of Number 10 – the windows are really quite large. The longer they stay there, the smaller the windows get. And I think it's very, very difficult for anyone to maintain that view of the world outside for more than about 10 years. There's also the more mundane problem that after 10 years, the back-benches are covered in people who you found wanting, and had to dump, and people who think they ought to be in the government, but who have been passed over.

HENNESSY

John Biffen called it 'The revenge of the unburied dead'.

TEBBIT

I think that was one of John's better remarks. I think he's absolutely right.

HENNESSY

If you had become Prime Minister, November 1990, what style of leadership would you have adopted? Collegiate but firm? How would you describe it?

TEBBIT

[*Laughing*] From the front, I suppose, is the answer. But always remembering what young men are taught at Sandhurst: that to lead is a huge privilege; that one owes a dual loyalty, first of all, of course, to Her Majesty the Queen, and secondly to those who you lead; and that the duty of a leader is always to make sure that the men and the horses are fed before he has dinner. And I think that's an essential part of leadership, that you should always be thinking about those who you are leading, because if not, they'll soon stop thinking very much about you.

HENNESSY

Who would you have made your Chancellor of the Exchequer and Foreign Secretary?

TEBBIT

I think probably Nigel Lawson would have been my Chancellor. Foreign Secretary – I don't really know. I think to a large extent I might have been my own Foreign Secretary. Whether that would have been for good or ill, I'm not sure.

HENNESSY

And the Foreign Office would have been stopped from representing foreigners in London?

TEBBIT

I think that certainly would have been the message that got to them! [*Laughs*]

HENNESSY

If you had made it, what statute can I give you?

TEBBIT

I think it would have been welfare reform, because I think that welfarism has become the curse of this country. When I like to pull the leg of left-wing audiences, I speak about it. I always pop in those words of Professor Beveridge in which he says that the period of time for which a man may draw unemployment benefit should be limited lest men become habituated to idleness.

HENNESSY

The Beveridge report of 1942.

TEBBIT

And that of course raises the most terrible shouts and yells, and I say, 'Well, not my words, Beveridge's words.' And had we enacted the original reforms in Attlee's day more in line with Beveridge, they would have stood the test of time better, because we've created a dependency culture, and that has really been a curse.

HENNESSY

Do you worry about your country and the fragilities home and abroad? Are you really anxious about our prospects?

TEBBIT

I am quite anxious about the future of the country for two reasons: one that, particularly in recent years, the Blairite, uncontrolled, uncounted and unlimited immigration has been more than our society could absorb, and therefore it's led to a fracturing of society in many ways. We can see that around us these days. That makes me anxious. Secondly, of course, is our relationship with our friends on the continent of Europe; that is again a great source of problems. And I think that fracturing of society, the culture of dependency and the problems of our relationship with Europe are the things which worry me most.

HENNESSY

And I think in early days, you were in favour of us joining the Common Market, as it was then called, because you were a free-trader.

TEBBIT

It was not so much that I was a free trader which propelled me into the European camp; but I found myself there for what I now realise were the same reasons as diplomats and members of major multinational companies. I had lost touch with the people of my own country, because I spent so much time abroad when I was flying; and I also, in that world, had found that my colleagues, other airline pilots, were a very congenial bunch, regardless of nationality; that we shared an enormous amount of views together, we were almost interchangeable really. And we also found that all the problems were ones which went across borders and could only be solved by trans-border authorities. Unconsciously, as in the case of diplomats and international business people, I had rather absorbed the idea that that went for everything. Gradually, as I spent more time in the Council of Ministers, where I made many friends and spent many, many congenial hours, as well as some deadly boring ones, I realised that the gulf of difference between us, because of our island history, and them, because of their continental history, was too great to be bridged. Curiously, I came to the view that we were more like the Germans than anybody else, and the more the EU seeks to expand, the less likely it is that it will be able to survive.

HENNESSY

Norman, I've always been intrigued by the contrast between the public image of Norman Tebbit and the private one, because those who know you to any degree know that you're jolly and self-ironic, but a lot of the public still see you as the *Spitting Image* puppet, the biker in the leather jacket. The toughie. Does that bother you?

TEBBIT

No, it never has. Partly because it's an image that has always appealed to young people, and that was very helpful to me. And secondly, when you think about it, that puppet was the one that always won. [*Hennessy laughs*] So there was an assumption that I was going to win the encounter, and indeed, I've always found, even when I've got mixed up with a bunch of drunken Millwall supporters on a Saturday night train from Merseyside, that they dealt with me with enormous courtesy and a great deal of fun.

HENNESSY

That's a very Norman Tebbit remark. How do you think you'd like history to remember you?

TEBBIT

I don't really mind; it'd be something to be remembered, wouldn't it? That's the first thing. I think, really, as a loyal lieutenant of the Prime Minister who stands out head and shoulders above any other in the late 20th century, except Churchill himself.

HENNESSY

How do you think you will be remembered?

TEBBIT

I think as a footnote, probably. [*Laughs*]

HENNESSY

A flavourful footnote, at the very least.

TEBBIT

Oh, I hope so, I hope so.

HENNESSY

Norman Tebbit, thank you very much indeed.

Neil Kinnock (Lord Kinnock)

Series 1, Episode 4, first broadcast 1 August 2013

Born 28 March 1942; **Educated** Lewis School,
Pengam; University College, Cardiff

MP (Labour) Bedwellty 1970–83; Islwyn 1983–95

Leader of the Labour Party and Leader of the Opposition,
1983–92. Member of the European Commission
1995–2004 (Vice President 1999–2004)

HENNESSY

With me today is a politician who so loved his party that he burnt up his personal prospects of the Premiership in the course of making Labour electable once more, under a different leader. He was, too, a politician who couldn't help putting passion and exuberance alongside the cold calculations needed for success at the very top of politics. Neil Kinnock, welcome.

KINNOCK

Thank you very much.

HENNESSY

Neil, if there was such a thing as a cradle of the wider Labour movement, not just the party but the trade unions, the Co-op, the Miners' Institutes with their fabulous libraries – it was your patch, crammed into those narrow South Walian valleys atop the black gold of the coal seams. Are you still, deep down, a child of that formation, a child of the valleys?

KINNOCK

In many ways, yes, and I think particularly in terms of loyalties and cultural encounters. Because the point was, it was a very cultured upbringing, which wasn't anything particularly special in working-class areas of that time, the late '40s, the '50s, when there were thriving choirs and operatic societies and thespian companies and visiting celebrity artists – who weren't people, then, off X-Factor, but were actually the finest operatic singers and concert performers in the world, which collectively, the workers in Tredegar by their weekly contributions to the Workmen's Hall – which was the huge theatre, beautifully appointed theatre – could actually afford to bring for one night on every third Sunday of the month throughout the winter months – and given the length of the winters in South Wales that used to mean about nine months of the year. And so, maybe to compensate for the narrowness of the valleys, there was a breadth of experience, obviously encouraged hugely by my parents and subsequently by the school, and those things I still relate to, and feel very much at home with. And I can go to the valleys now – which have changed *hugely* of course, and in some ways not for the better because of the economic battering that they have had over the last 30, 40 years – and feel that I've been away for 20 minutes.

HENNESSY

There was another side to the culture of those valleys in those days: the greatest poet of post-war politics, Aneurin Bevan. And I think you used to go as a boy with your dad up to Waun-y-Pound where his memorial is now, still between Tredegar and Ebbw Vale, to listen to his open-air meetings. That must have been, for you, given your formation, and the sort of chap you are, that must have been like a shot of electricity.

KINNOCK

It was wonderful. And you're right to describe Nye as a poet of politics because although he could be, when required, clinical and forensic, both in debate and in the way in which he established a National Health Service, was a brilliant housing minister, which people forget about, was a great local-government minister …

HENNESSY

The Ministry of Health did Housing and Local Government as well, which everybody forgets …

KINNOCK

Absolutely. And he turned his hand to the immensely practical and beneficial, benevolent indeed, enterprise of creating the health service. And so what was great about Bevan, wasn't simply his poetry, his oratory, which was obviously world-class, and maybe the best encountered in the century because it wasn't confined to open-air meetings at Waun-y-Pound above Tredegar, he was brilliant in committee, he was wonderful in Parliament, and he was great on the conference platform too. I only heard Nye speak twice in the open air; on other occasions it was in halls, particularly in the Workmen's Hall whenever he was in trouble, [*laughing*] which was fairly frequent, he would come to his constituency and not address a closed general committee meeting or even a trades council, where I also heard him speak when I was a young socialist delegate – but to 1,800 to 2,000 people packed into the Workmen's Hall, with a Tannoy system broadcasting to a few thousand more outside. And he would speak for an hour, he would use sophisticated language, he would make Biblical allusions, he would use snatches of Shakespeare or Wordsworth, and people would thrill to his every word. And by the time they left, they understood why he was in trouble, and they also understood why they were on his side. [*Laughs*]

HENNESSY

One of the great divisions between politicians, temperamental types, is between poets and plumbers, and from what you're saying about Nye Bevan, he could be a plumber when he had to be, but we all remember the poetry. Are you, Neil, more poetry than plumbing? Are you any good at the plumbing? Or does the poetry always intrude, trump everything else, because you can be no other?

KINNOCK

The people who worked with me thought I gave too much attention to plumbing; I would answer them by saying, unless the reorganisation of the Labour Party and the alteration of our policies is led from the top and undertaken in detail in every nook and cranny, it's not going to get done, and we can't afford to skimp. I need to assert my authority in the most minuscule details, absurdly sometimes, in order to win an argument, get a change, secure an amendment. So my preference is for poetry, I make no bones about that, and maybe my talent, such as it is, is more for poetry than for plumbing. But the plumbing had to be done, and when faced with that, the general assessment is, I think, that I made a pretty good job of it! [*Laughs*]

HENNESSY

We'll come back to what I think you once called your mid-life crisis, ie leading the Labour Party, in a minute. [*Laughs*]

KINNOCK

Yes, [*laughing*] few people can so accurately, almost to the minute, define their midlife crisis – mine began on the 2nd of October 1983 and finished on the 18th of July, 1992, and after that and before that I've had a wonderful life! [*They laugh*]

HENNESSY

When did you first think of becoming an MP? How old were you? Can you remember where and when, and what triggered it?

KINNOCK

I think it was, as a real prospect or possibility, a *real* ambition, after Glenys and I got married and we'd moved to what turned out to be the constituency of Bedwellty. We got the house there because it was midway between where Glenys worked and where I worked, and I discovered that the Member of Parliament, a very well-respected man called Harold Finch, was not in his late 50s, as I thought, but in his late 60s but nevertheless secure and unlikely to change. I will say, because of what people said to me, I *did* think 'This could occur in the next 10 years', not necessarily for Bedwellty, though the conditions were propitious. If anything, the prospect of becoming a Member of Parliament loomed larger in Merthyr Tydfil, where the Member of Parliament was S.O. Davies, rather than in Bedwellty simply because of the acquaintances I had, and the work I was engaged in was much more in the Merthyr valley, and in the town of Merthyr.

HENNESSY

Because you were a Workers Educational Association teacher, which of course you loved – that job was made for you.

KINNOCK

Oh, it was wonderful – in terms of the students, who were an inspiration; in terms of the people that I worked for – there was a genius called DT Guy, David Thomas Guy, an ex-coal miner, who'd got his way into university and graduated, and he was the District Secretary who appointed me, and I adored the man, he was a wonderful man. But for the accident of being elected to Parliament at 28 years of age, I would have continued happily for decades.

HENNESSY

But Finch decides to retire at the next election, which turns out to be June 1970, and you win Bedwellty in the valleys, classic Labour seat, huge majority, career there for life if you wanted it. And you make a mark very quickly in the House of Commons.

KINNOCK

Yes, I think ginger hair and a facility with jokes helped. And over the years my capacity for manufacturing jokes has landed me in some difficulty on occasion, but generally speaking it's been employed to make a serious point with a degree of wit. Maybe people heard that and caught on. The other thing is, as others have reflected since, I was certainly on the left, in the Bevanite tradition, and a huge supporter of my beloved comrade Michael Foot, but I nevertheless had no appetite at all for avid, sectarian posturing, and one or two of my colleagues on the left tended in that direction.

HENNESSY

That's very tactfully put; there were more than one or two in the early '70s, as you well know.

KINNOCK

Well, there were a few. They irritated me, and I could not forbear to tell them! [*Laughs*]

HENNESSY

You went into the Shadow Cabinet after Mrs Thatcher won in '79, and Labour's in opposition, and I think the public as a whole probably got a vivid sense of you – they had a sense of you already, because you're very good in the media, but I think it was the speech you made two nights before the poll in 1983 that did it: 'If Margaret Thatcher wins on Thursday, I warn you not to be ordinary; I warn you not to be young; I warn you not to fall ill; I warn you not to be old.' I think that's when you made your real imprint into the velcro of collective memory. It was as if everything that was in your formation boiled out, because you knew you were going to lose, big-time. Was it, as Nye Bevan would have called it, an 'emotional spasm', Neil, or did you calculate it?

KINNOCK

I did an unusual thing for that speech. I wrote it. Because I hardly ever, up until that point, had written speeches. I wrote it sitting in the back of a car that Glenys was driving down the M4 to finish the week campaigning in and around South Wales, and I felt these lines coming to me and scribbled them down. And the first 20 minutes of writing just flowed out. And then I stopped and read it back to myself, and read it to Glenys as she was driving, and she said, 'Hmm – you've gone in for blank verse.' So I wrote the second part of it consciously as blank verse. I decided to continue the rhythm of 'I warn you'. And it was a speech of defiance and, as you suggest, desperation. And I think you're right that that sort of made me recognisable, very rapidly, and then of course it was almost immediately followed by the leadership election campaign after Michael resigned in the wake of the electoral defeat.

HENNESSY

A future young historian of the Labour movement, say 30 years on, might say, 'Neil Kinnock had the perfect skill set to be a man of 1945' – the 1945 election, that combination of your formation of the valleys, the flesh of the flesh of the wider Labour movement, the style of rhetoric – that Neil would have been winner takes all in a 1945 context, but by '83, both the country and the world, and the nature of the media, and the nature of parliamentary politics had changed. Do you think there's anything in that?

KINNOCK

I think there's something in it. Yes, it is true that the politics had changed. We had the novelty of Margaret Thatcher, and what by 1983 she had become, and continued increasingly to be in the years after that. The media was changing, and that had a certain effect. But what I was trying to appeal to is the basic sense of community of interest in employment, the development of the economy for future requirements, the production of wealth and its fair distribution, and the expansion of opportunity for those who were willing to make the commitment and work hard. Now they're fairly fundamental, eternal objectives for any progressive, democratic politician, and I criticise myself for not delivering those arguments to the public in a way that was sufficiently appealing *and* reassuring to win eventually in '92.

In '87 I knew we didn't have a chance. My disappointment was that we didn't manage to win more seats, because that would have given us a different basis for attack in 1992. Many of the margins were very, very narrow indeed, but nevertheless, if you come second, that's no good. And '87 was in the least propitious circumstances, so I knew we were going to get very badly beaten then; but I really do criticise myself for not amending the message, or sharpening it, or making whatever change was necessary in order to ensure that it persuaded people that they were part of the community that would benefit from and contribute to this general advancement of people of all backgrounds in every class. And there's nobody else to blame for that.

HENNESSY

The gods of politics can be wrathful gods, and they were very wrathful on you in your first years as leader of the Labour Party, in terms of both the miners' strike and the Militant Tendency. The miners' strike, Neil, must have cut right into your core because it's about the communities that you lived and breathed in. Looking back, was there any way you could have shoved Arthur Scargill into having a national vote? The whole thing turned on that. This enormous strike, the vulnerability of those communities to pit closures and so on – you felt that as much as anybody could feel it, and yet here was this union leader, who in effect was running against you and the wider Labour movement – many people have thought – not having the national ballot before taking them all out, and splitting the miners depending on which coal field you were in. I mean that must have been unendurable for you, and it went on month after month after month.

KINNOCK

It was appalling. Appalling. And the destitution – that's the only appropriate word – of what I saw in the pit communities, with people entirely dependent upon the collective effort and charity contributions to put food on the table for their children … that was searing. As far as persuading, where Scargill was concerned I knew that was beyond all possibility. What I criticise myself for is not, as early as possible in the strike, saying this cannot achieve anything but misery without a national ballot. And what that would have done was give me the political space to confine the arguments to the case for and against pit closures. Instead of that, by not doing that, I was pulled into the vortex of the dispute itself, and it was easy for my opponents in politics and the press to caricature me as being an apologist for Scargillism, which God knows I never was.

The reason that I didn't make that assertion early in the dispute, either you have a ballot or you will be beaten in conditions of national disunity – is that the people I represented at senior trade-union level, and at neighbour level, at family level, were people who had already made months of sacrifice in the work-to-rule, lost lots of weekly pay, and were in favour of a ballot, but knew that nobody was going to listen to them unless and until they withdrew their labour. And these people, giving the finest example of loyalty, bravery, solidarity, would have been kicked in the face if I had lectured them at the beginning of the strike.

Even then I was caught unawares, as everybody else was, by the fact that a specially convened conference of the miners, over

Easter weekend in 1984, *appeared* to be called for two reasons: one, to change the constitution of the NUM so that a majority of 50% plus one vote would be enough for a national strike, and that led everybody, including me, to believe that the immediate consequence of that would be to have the ballot. Well, they certainly passed the constitutional change, but we didn't even receive a motion to have the ballot. And those few weeks before that, when I lived in expectation – together with everybody else, *including a lot of striking miners* – that the great change was going to come, was the period in which I should have made it clear: it's a ballot or it's defeat. Because of course if a ballot had taken place, the whole circumstances in which the strike took place would have changed. It would have been much, much shorter. Sensible people in the government would have got the NCB to the negotiating table, and a rational, genuine trade unionist leading the NUM, which Scargill wasn't of course, would have come to compromise terms which is the essence of the purpose and strength of trade union-ism. And it would have been done honourably, with a minimum of harm, and changed the political condition substantially. That's all 'if' and 'maybe'; the reality was vile and the reality was miserable.

HENNESSY

Do you think Arthur Scargill had you in his sights, as much as he had Mrs Thatcher? That not only was it a political strike against a Conservative government, but against a certain type of Labour leadership?

KINNOCK

Maybe. He would subsequently claim that. But most of the months of the strike were months in which what he wanted to do was have me to blame for not "winning", in inverted commas, the strike. He wanted to be able to claim that it was the political weakness and treachery of the leadership of the Labour Party that wouldn't call for a general strike nationally, if you've ever heard anything so absurd, that had really brought the downfall of the miners. Fortunately the miners are too sensible to believe that, so even though the claims were made by a few in the ultra-left, and Scargillites, I've never, ever encountered, on any coal field, at any time, any rank-and-file miner or lodge official who said that kind of thing to me. So Scargill utterly failed in that. But the worst failure, of course, was paid for by countless pit communities and youngsters and men who were out of work for years on end, and families that were desperately impoverished.

HENNESSY

The other great absorber of time and your nervous energy was the Militant Tendency.

KINNOCK

[*Laughing*] Yes.

HENNESSY

The Trotskyites within the Labour Party practising all these dreadful tactics of entryism. And it took ages for you to sort them out, not until you made that amazing speech at the Labour Party conference in '85, about the grotesque spectacle of redundancy notices being given out in Liverpool, Derek Hatton and Co were running that[1]. When you think about it, Neil, the Conservatives were dominating the political scene, and you had not only the miners' strike but what some would call the enemy within the Labour Party. I mean, what a double-headed blow for you, even though in the end it was the making of you in many ways with a wider section of the country – that speech, which was one of the greatest Party Conference speeches anybody can remember, in '85. But my heavens there was bloodshed on the way, wasn't there.

---

1 Derek Hatton was deputy leader of Liverpool Council and a member of Militant, a Trotskyite organisation.

KINNOCK

Oh, there was; and it would have come a year earlier, but for the miners' strike. One of the things I was determined to do when I became elected leader, one of the reasons why I valued the very large majority that I got in that contest, was that I knew I needed all of the strength within the movement that I could get to take these people out. Because it was no good pulling the trigger unless there was going to be a kill, if I can speak figuratively. But I couldn't do it in the conference of '84 because of the miners' strike. At that time, for reasons I understood, the Labour movement, the whole Labour movement, was utterly preoccupied with the dispute and everything that went with it. And any attempt to try and focus attention on the wilful damage being done by the entrist Militant tendency would have just skimmed off the surface. And so the greatest test for me was keeping my powder dry for a further 12 months, which was far from easy, especially when I had leaders of Liverpool City Council [*laughs*] idiotically coming into my office and telling me that with a conjunction of defiance in Liverpool by the Militant-led council and the [*Liverpudlian accent*] circum-stances generated by the miners' strike, [*back to his accent*] and a new consciousness that was arising in the working class, that if I called for a general strike I would bring down Margaret Thatcher. They sat on the other side of the table, with me with a few members of the Shadow Cabinet there, listening to this, and I said, 'There's more chance of me riding down Lime Street on a rhinoceros than any of this happening'. And of course that was further evidence of my deviationist treachery.

Anyway, I had to hang on and get to the conference, and it had to be at the conference because that was the only place to plant it right between their eyes. Even then, the difficult part was to come, because denouncing them is one thing; making it effective by expelling them from the Labour Party was entirely different, espe-cially with a constitution that was built by a very tolerant party for tolerant and well-meaning people. So I had to use this constitution whilst fully observing the requirements of natural justice in order to arraign these people, against whom we had evidence before us, and expel them from the Labour Party. And it took hours and hours, and days and days, with television cameras parked outside Labour Party headquarters, and these clowns posturing and eventually being expelled on the basis of the evidence scrupulously observed. And it took us altogether with the first group of Liverpool militants about three or four months to get rid of them. And then there were more expulsions around the country, and we changed the constitution – what I was saying earlier about being a plumber – changed the constitution in detail, and went through the whole paraphernalia, so that we got a party which was a very unhealthy place for entrists or for people with purposes that were fundamentally divergent from those of the democratic, socialist, social democratic Labour Party.

HENNESSY

There was one other aspect of turning the Labour Party in new directions, which I think was difficult for you, because you naturally loathe the possibility of nuclear war. I know everybody does, but you took the unilateralist side when you were a young man, and the Labour Party for the bulk of the '80s, until you managed to amend it, was committed to that. And you suffered in many interviews from this always being brought up, and indeed I think in '83 you said that if you were Prime Minister you couldn't really authorise nuclear release, you just couldn't retaliate, whatever had happened. Now, that must have been particularly difficult for you, given that it was deep within you.

KINNOCK

Yes, because in many ways plain common sense was on its side. The whole thesis of mutually assured destruction requires very sensible and humane people to sustain the idea that there are circumstances in which they just might use it, maybe even as a first strike, very definitely in retaliation. And I've actually never met anybody, with the possible exception of Mrs Thatcher, but maybe not even her, who behind their eyes really acknowledged the reality that they would use the terminal weapon. And I thought, for long periods, that it was better to offer leadership that was based on the acknowledgment of that truth than the alternative. Experience taught me that it didn't matter how valid the arguments were, how impressive the facts and figures were, how excessive the expenditure is, how appalling the possibility was of use of these weapons – no one other than about 25%, on a good day 27% of the electorate, was ever going to listen to it. And so I had to say to the Labour Party when I changed the policy – and it was a rugged activity, it required not the winning of an argument but the displacement of an almost religious commitment that ran across the movement – I had to say to them, 'I've been where you've been on the picket line. I've been where you *haven't* been in the White House, in the Élysée, in the Kremlin, and I can tell you: not only can you not persuade people on the street, the counterparts don't even understand what you're saying.'

HENNESSY

In the Élysée, in the White House, in the Kremlin.

KINNOCK

And I said, on the basis of that experience, I'm telling you, no. I will not persist with the policy as it exists; I will only lead the party if we change the policy in the way that I've drafted. And we secured the agreement of the National Executive Committee, and a few months later the Labour Party Conference, and made a different manifesto stance. And that leadership was necessary because if it hadn't been done we would have doomed the Labour Party to maybe decades more out of office simply because it was an examination by the public, not of the validity or lack of validity of the argument about the nuclear deterrent and the readiness to use it, but the fundamental trustworthiness of political parties seeking to become the government. And to pass the test of trust-worthiness you had to say there could be circumstances in which the weapon might have to be used and it was wise, therefore, for our country to retain the weapon. And we made substantial gains on the basis of that; unfortunately, not enough to win.

HENNESSY

Looking back, do you think it's inevitable that in the wider sweep of British political history you will be seen as a man of immense energy and commitment and courage, who immolated himself to create tarmac for somebody else to get into Number 10 under the Labour colours; that you paved somebody else's way, that somebody had to, and it just turned out to be you.

KINNOCK

I'm very reluctant to accept that description, though I know it's used, and it probably will be used, I know. It'd always be interesting, wouldn't it, to peep at your own obituaries. [*Laughs*]

HENNESSY

This is the nearest you're going to get, Neil.

KINNOCK

Yes, well I've written a few! But nevertheless: I strove to win. When I lost in 1992, by what Bob Worcester told me was twelve hundred and forty votes, which is the combined lowest 11 Conservative majorities, so it was pretty close out of 25 million votes, I was deeply downcast until it became apparent that the Labour Party had changed fundamentally in a more progressive and a more successful direction and there was therefore a possibility that what we'd achieved between '83 and '92 was going to be the foundation for substantial success. So I take some satisfaction from that. And despite all the miserable times, as my children occasionally remind me there were *some* fulfilling experiences that came as a result of occupying that position over those years. To see Nelson Mandela, just weeks after he came out of Pollsmoor jail, at the invitation of Ingvar Carlsson the then Swedish Prime Minister and a very dear friend of mine, to go to Stockholm to meet Mandela, to have hours with him, to be *recognised* by him, incredibly – because he'd been looking at pictures of myself and Glenys speaking in Trafalgar Square. They were nailed up on his cell wall. Those kinds of experiences would not have come about in that way. To go to Berlin a week after the wall came down, speak at the SPD congress in honour of Willy Brandt's – another great friend of mine – 75th birthday; I wouldn't have traded that for anything.

HENNESSY

There was somebody else, slightly surprising, who said good things about you, in terms of the wider historical sweep. I think Mrs Thatcher once said to you, 'History will be kind to you', didn't she?

KINNOCK

She did, actually. She wrote a kind and courteous note, that was dated the day that I stopped being leader of the Labour Party, and I was touched by that. She still addressed me as 'Mr Kinnock'. [*Laughs*] And I reciprocated. But that was a civilised element of otherwise, honestly, vituperative politics. And if we keep that mixture of civilised people being moved by convictions, asserting themselves passionately, but within a determinately democratic setting, that we seek to strengthen, I don't think we'll go far wrong.

HENNESSY

Kenneth Morgan, the great historian of 20th century politics, particularly Welsh politics, and political leaders, once said about Nye Bevan, 'Like Lloyd George he was an artist in the use of power', terrific phrase. Do you think, Neil, that is what you wanted to be if you'd made it to Number 10? What would you have done, what's the style and the flavour of the Kinnock Premiership we never had?

KINNOCK

The only purpose of getting democratic power is to use it for the enlargement of people's opportunities and the further strengthening of democracy; and consequently, I would, for instance, have an explicit national-health and community-care tax, whose product went only to the NHS and community care. And it would have meant modifying the so-called standard rate of income tax, and it would have encountered the resistance of the Treasury – but we would have done it, and the NHS would have been assured permanently of buoyant finance.

HENNESSY

So quite a chunk of taxation would have been hypothecated, to use the technical term.

KINNOCK

Indeed. And I think that, in the modern world, where people need to see a direct connection between their expenditure and what is returned for that, we will move towards a much more specific relationship between what you pay and what you get. It won't be confined to health, it I think will extend to higher education, especially in the wake of the unfortunate changes that have taken place in this century with higher-education funding. But the buoyancy of that, including expenditure on research, is essential. And it can't afford to take second place to some other forms of expenditure and so I think democratic politicians are going to have to be able to demonstrate that the quality of what is being received by the community is in a direct connection with the quantity and quality of investment being put in.

HENNESSY

For all your word-power, Neil, and you do feel as a natural European now, you didn't when you were younger, but you do now …

KINNOCK

Well, I did – I just didn't like what I thought the Common Market was. I was wrong.

HENNESSY

But you're a natural European now. Why is it that nobody has managed to sing a song of Europe, as it were, to the British people, the wider British people, particularly the younger ones? Why is it we have this persistent emotional deficit with the European community?

KINNOCK

Some of it is to do with the very widespread political habit, not confined to this country, of describing any advance or success or plus in the European Union as 'their' accomplishment, and anything that is disagreeable as 'the fault of the bureaucrats of Brussels'. And cumulatively, of course, over decades, that takes on a life of its own. In addition, I don't think the argument has ever been assiduously made – and I mean decade-in and decade-out – that in the modern world, if countries want to effectively possess and use power, they increasingly have to do it collectively. And what we are doing in the European Union is subscribing to a pool of power, some of the powers previously retained in the nation state, in order that collectively in economic terms, environmental terms, in combating crime, in movement of people, in research and development, in a host of other areas where real authority to achieve outcomes has passed beyond the borders of states, that in return for pooling some power, we're actually accumulating a greater authority over our own destiny. That is the truth, it's been understood for many, many years, but it's never been effectively explained in a way that secured generation-to-generation understanding. Maybe now's the time to start again doing that, because with every year passes, with globalisation, greater integration, greater interdependence, not just of the European continent but the whole damn world, that reality of acting together in order to act effectively is becoming more and more sharp, and more and more evident. And we've already got the amenity of the European Union to accomplish those things. Other parts of the world are trying to build similar models. And the last thing we should do is put our future in that in any form of question whatsoever.

HENNESSY

What's it like having a daughter-in-law who's a successful centre-left politician in Denmark, is indeed the prime minister? This must be a peculiar satisfaction, even though you didn't make it in.

KINNOCK

Oh, it's wonderful, and she's a wonderful woman. Helle is a daughter to us, and happily both of our children and our son- and daughter-in-law are great friends to each other, and with us. We don't find ourselves talking such a great deal of politics, because my view is, and I think hers is too, that there are wider areas for enjoyable exchange: holidays and kids.

HENNESSY

What trace would you like to leave on history?

KINNOCK

I'd like to be remembered as a tall, slim man, with a deep voice [*Peter laughs*] who gave up the Premiership after 25 years. [*Both laugh*]

HENNESSY

What trace do you think you *will* leave on history?

KINNOCK

Who thinks in these terms? Do you think in those terms?

HENNESSY

Well, I think senior politicians do, a lot of them, Neil.

KINNOCK

I think it's important that anybody who stands for democratic office, certainly at national parliamentary level, is conscious of the fact that they are going to try to act in ways that have an effect on history. To fail to understand that is to fail to comprehend the nature of the duty and the task. But those politicians that I've encountered who think of themselves as history-makers, are very drab indeed. Very superficial. They perforce are obsessed with tomorrow's headlines and they will drift before the wind in order to make their place in history. There are very, very few people who are genuine history makers, who have performed acts with a deliberate intention of making history. They have done it either because it was the right thing, or because they *thought* it was the right thing, not because they were going to achieve a different theatrical review.

HENNESSY

Neil Kinnock, thank you very much indeed.

KINNOCK

Thank you.

John Major (Sir John Major)

Series 2, Episode 1, first broadcast 13 August 2014

Born 29 March 1943; **Educated** Rutlish Grammar
School, Merton, South London

MP (Conservative) Huntingdonshire 1979–83; Huntingdon 1983–2001

Assistant Government Whip, 1983–84; Government Whip
1984–85; Parliamentary Secretary for Social Security, Department
of Health and Social Security, 1985–86; Minister of State,
DHSS, 1986–87; Chief Secretary to the Treasury, 1987–89;
Foreign and Commonwealth Secretary, 1989; Chancellor of
the Exchequer, 1989–90; Leader of the Conservative Party,
First Lord of the Treasury and Prime Minister, 1990–97.

Autobiography *The Autobiography*, 1999

HENNESSY

With me today is one of our unexpected Prime Ministers. On the
evening he captured the Premiership, he reflected on how great the
three-mile journey had been from his boyhood in Coldharbour
Lane, Brixton to Number 10 Downing Street. His colleagues say
he opened his first Cabinet meeting with the words, 'Who would
have believed it?' Sir John Major, welcome. It was a long way from
Brixton to Number 10: it's an extraordinary story of a suburban
upbringing and tough times in Brixton to the highest office in the

land. When were the seeds of ambition first planted in you? When were you first aware that you wanted to do something big in public and political life?

MAJOR

I think probably about the age of 13. And I think what influenced me most were what Harold Macmillan would have called, 'Events, dear boy, events'. It was what I saw and what I experienced that made me realise that I would like to take part in public life to see if I could change some things. I always had a fascination for history, and the first time I ever went in the House of Commons – at the invitation of a Labour MP actually, Marcus Lipton, the Member for Brixton – I felt that there is a special atmosphere in that building, and it reaches out and grabs you. And I thought to myself, this is where I'd like to work.

HENNESSY

But where does the Conservative impulse come from? It's a crude way of looking at it, but so many do see it that way in our class-obsessed country – you were from the wrong side of the tracks, to use an American phrase, and yet you were in no doubt that you were a Conservative, that this was the way to get those beneficial changes.

MAJOR

At the time, when I was 12, 13, 14, we lived in Brixton, five members of the family in two rooms and a little landing upon which we cooked, and the washroom three floors down. And the Labour Party in Lambeth were very big-hearted; their attitude generally was, 'Yes, you are in difficulties, and in due course we will help you, but be patient'. And the Conservative Party said to me, we'd like to open up avenues of opportunity for you to change your own circumstances, and those of your own family. And of the two philosophies, there was no doubt which one appealed to me. So I was by instinct Conservative. I'm not an ideologue in any way, and what attracts me is what pragmatically can be done not whether it meets some ideological test or other.

In your memoirs, you have a very vivid section about your hatred of class obsessions in our dear country. You said, 'I was in earnest about classlessness; I wanted to say that the subtle calibrations of scorn in which this country rejoices, the endless putting-downs and belittlings, so instinctive that we don't notice ourselves doing them, are awful.' Now, there's passion and there's pain in there. Were you patronised as a young man from South London in that old Conservative Party, by the grander figures?

You see there's an assumption there that it was the Conservative Party that was being patronising. And if that was so, why would I join them? In fact, it wasn't so much that, it was more the way that life behaved. The fact that there were glass ceilings on opportunity for many people, depending upon their background; that there were different social values applied to people who had blue-collar jobs, and people who had white-collar jobs. There was a different social value placed on immigration. I saw immigrants at very close quarters in the 1950s; they shared my house, they were my neighbours. I played with them as boys. And I didn't see people who'd come here just to benefit from our social system, I saw people with the guts and the drive to travel half way across the world in many cases, to better themselves and their families, and I think that's a very Conservative instinct, to do that. That's what I saw. And it was things like that – and also the fear I saw amongst many people who had nothing, perhaps unsophisticated people as well. I saw a fear of officialdom among them. And it was things like that made me think: there are changes that can be made, and they can better be made from a Conservative attitude than from any other attitude.

HENNESSY

In those formative years you seemed very at ease with Harold Macmillan and Rab Butler and Iain Macleod, you're a classic one-nation formulation Conservative. And Napoleon used to say, if you want to understand a man or woman in authority, think of the world as it was when they were 20 or 21. And you are from that era, that post-war, relatively consensual era of concerned Conservatism. Is that the key to John Major, really?

MAJOR

Certainly I felt comfortable with it – I much prefer consensus to disagreement; if you can reach consensus, so much the better. And certainly of the politicians of those days I think above all it was Iain Macleod who most attracted my attention as a young teenager. Firstly because of what he said, which was uplifting, and secondly because of the way he said it, which was compelling. He had some form of paralysis of the neck which kept his head absolutely unmoving, and he had a voice like a ringing bell, and it was inspiring to listen to. And certainly as an 11, 12, 13, 14-year-old, if I could hear Iain Macleod speak, I would, and I drank in every word.

HENNESSY

You're a man of immense application and tenacity, but why didn't you work at school, at Rutlish Grammar School? Why did it all come later? I know people fire up at different points in their intellectual life, but it's a bit of a mystery, that, John.

MAJOR

Well, not to me. Circumstances at home weren't easy. My father was very sick, and was plainly at the beginning of dying; my mother was very sick; there were lots of domestic problems. I had to travel from Brixton to Wimbledon each day. There were difficulties that sat in the forefront of my mind, far more than studying. And so I suppose, rather in the way young people do, I withdrew from what

I should have been doing, which was studying, and concentrated on other matters. I knew I was doing it, and I knew I was foolish in doing it, but I couldn't not do it. And then the moment I left school, I knew I had to study, and I had to make up for that.

HENNESSY

And you certainly did, and you came in, in the great rush of new Conservative MPs in May 1979. A pretty rapid rise: you were in the Whips' Office first of all, and record has it you had the most furious row with Mrs Thatcher, quite early on.

MAJOR

That's absolutely true.

HENNESSY

Not entirely a career-enhancing move, one would have thought.

MAJOR

Well, it turned out to be so actually because she is an extraordinary set of contradictions. These days when you talk of Margaret Thatcher, you have to draw a distinction between the Margaret Thatcher of legend promoted by her opponents and by her adherents, and the real Margaret Thatcher, the flesh-and-blood Margaret Thatcher that I knew. It's certainly true that we had a colossal row. It was the fashion in those days for the Chief Whip to invite the Prime Minister for dinner once a year with the whips, and she came, and after two minutes she had exhausted the social chat-chat that she loathed so much. And so we sat down to dinner and John Wakeham said, well, the economy's central …

HENNESSY

He was the Chief Whip …

MAJOR

John was the Chief Whip at the time. 'The economy's central', he said, 'I'll ask the Treasury whip, John Major, to talk about what the Party's view is.' So I told her, and the Party's view wasn't what she wished to hear, and so she decided, rather than enter into debate, that she would shoot the messenger, which she attempted to do in spectacular style, and I responded in equal style, saying that this may not be what she wished to hear, but that's what the party thought, and that was what I was going to tell her. And the argument went on for some time. And one or two of the Whips came up to me afterwards and said, well, that was a short career. And the following day I was the whip on duty sitting on the green benches in a sparse House, and Margaret came and sat next to me and said, "I've been thinking about what you said last night, we ought to have a further meeting to discuss it". And she went into the Whips' Office and convened a further meeting. And about three weeks later she had a reshuffle, and appointed me junior minister at the Department of Health and Social Security, in the job in which she herself had started, and which she thought was a good learning job. So there's a curious contradiction. She behaved pretty unreasonably in the conversation and then afterwards the other side of Margaret appeared. She didn't say 'I was wrong', but she put right what had gone wrong, and then promoted me.

HENNESSY

Mrs Thatcher must have seen something very special in you from that extraordinary set-to. She said you were the one that she wanted to succeed the night you took over; but did she realise that you were quite so right-through One Nation? Did you think she was misreading you, and did you allow her to misread you?

MAJOR

No I didn't. I mean, if she did misread me I'm puzzled as to how that happened, because both as Chief Secretary and as Chancellor, and briefly as Foreign Secretary, a glorious 94 days in which we went to war with no one, I saw a great deal of Margaret Thatcher one-to-one – and we didn't always agree. And we did have a relationship where I could say to her what I thought; I didn't have to temper what I thought, and I *didn't* temper what I thought. So I find it difficult to understand how she could have misunderstood what my views were, because they were expressed often enough.

HENNESSY

Do you think you were ready for the Premiership in 1990? Would you like to have done longer time in one of the big offices of state?

MAJOR

Yes, I would.

HENNESSY

Why was that? What did you think you were missing still?

MAJOR

I think I was missing the fact that the longer you have been in government, the more experience you have. I would have preferred it if I had become Prime Minister a few years later. I think that would have been easier in terms of how I felt about it, and I think it would have been easier in terms of the experience I was able to bring to the job. But if the ball comes your way, you grab it. There's nothing else you can do.

HENNESSY

When you become Prime Minister, the whole weight of special responsibilities fall upon you, including the most awesome one, which I've written a little bit about, which is having to do the nuclear weapons stuff, the 'last resort' letters. And I was very struck when David Cameron told me, on-the-record, that when he had to write about what he wanted from beyond the grave if we were wiped out by a nuclear bolt from the blue, he told me he called you in and asked for your advice. It's the most awesome thing that falls upon a new Prime Minister, so how did you prepare yourself for it, and later how did you help David Cameron prepare for writing down those extraordinary letters to go on the submarines?

MAJOR

It is a shock. The first time I realised that I was going to have to write post-Armageddon instructions to our four Trident submarines[1] was when the Cabinet Secretary told me. And it is quite an extraordinary introduction to the Premiership. And I remember I went away over the weekend, and I thought about it a lot, and it was one of the most difficult things I ever had to do, to write those instructions – the essence of them being that, if the UK is wiped out but its Trident submarines are at sea with their weaponry, what should they then do with their weaponry? And eventually I reached a conclusion, and I set it out, and I talked to David about that. I'm not going to say what I said, but we discussed the parameters of it, and I left him to make his own decision, as he did.

HENNESSY

Soon after you became Prime Minister – actually, straight away, given the condition of the Middle East – you were engaged in the run-up to the first Gulf War.

MAJOR

A few days before the war started, I went to Saudi Arabia to meet the then-exiled Kuwaiti royal family, and reassured them that Britain would be with the United States, because their closeness to the United Kingdom was – and is – remarkable. And I also went to visit the troops. And there were several things that

---

1 In fact, the letters were destined for the inner safes of Royal Navy Polaris submarines in 1990.

struck me about that. The first was how young they were. And I remember standing on a tank talking to thousands of them, and I knew, though they did not, that the war would begin on the 16th of January, and this was just a few days earlier. And as I spoke to them, all these boys sitting there, their faces metamorphosed into those of my son, whose 16th birthday was the date at which war began. A year or so older and he could have been part of them. And all their faces morphed into my son's when I was talking to them, and that is a memory of war I've never forgotten.

HENNESSY

There's a paradox in your Premiership in the early years, when, as you like to put it, you felt you were living in sin with the electorate because you hadn't got your own majority, which you did get against expected political form in '92, but then troubles came in battalions in late summer and early autumn of 1992. And so you had your majority, but the gods of politics can be very malign, and they dumped on you, John, didn't they? It must be quite painful for you, looking back, to see that paradox, because once you were no longer living in sin with the electorate your party erupted around you. Black Wednesday and the European question asserting itself again ...

MAJOR

Of course the party changed in 1992. A large number of the last remnants of the post-war generation were succeeded, those who had been in the war and who thought anything was better than having another European war – they had lived through one, and had memories of the first earlier in the century, and they were prepared to make accommodations to bring Europe together so there could never again be another European war. But they were succeeded by new young group of Conservatives who had grown up in a much more ideological age, with a much more ideological bent, and without the historic memory of the war and its immediate aftermath. So the parliamentary party that was so difficult after 1992 was a different, significantly different, parliamentary party from the party that had existed throughout the '70s, '80s, and the early part of the '90s. And then what significantly changed things was the collapse of sterling, falling out of the exchange rate mechanism.

HENNESSY

16th of September, 1992. A day which you'll always remember.

MAJOR

16th of September, 1992. I'm unlikely to forget it. [*Both laugh*] But of course, the background to it *was* forgotten. Why did we go in to the exchange rate mechanism? Why did Margaret Thatcher sign up to the exchange rate mechanism? And she did. *And – she – did.*

HENNESSY

You persuaded her and Douglas Hurd, the Foreign Secretary, did.

MAJOR

We talked to her, and she was persuaded. And she wasn't, as some have said, persuaded with a pistol held to her head. I will tell you *exactly* why Margaret agreed to go into the exchange rate mechanism: because as she came to the end of her Premiership, we were suffering the recession that so often follows a boom. There had been a boom in the late 1980s and we were now heading into the recession. Inflation, on the day I became Prime Minister, was very nearly 10%. Unemployment was soaring. Interest rates were 14% and we were undoubtedly heading for a deep recession. Now, Margaret cared about inflation. It hurt the people that she knew. She wanted to bring inflation down. And *that* is why she decided we would go into the exchange rate mechanism, because every time in her political life and mine we had had an anti-inflationary policy, the government had given way when it got difficult, and the exchange rate mechanism produced a clear external discipline to bring inflation down.

And so concerned about that was she that she actually wished to go into the exchange rate mechanism at a more punitive exchange rate than the one we chose. So the argument that Margaret was unwillingly pushed into the exchange rate mechanism is utterly, utterly false. But then of course, when we crashed out, it was taken by the Eurosceptics as a classic reason to pile in on Europe, on every conceivable front, and that of course is what happened. It was a great calamity, a political calamity that we came out. What is frustrating about that is that we had already been discussing privately within government – I had been discussing with the policy unit and others – how we could come out of the exchange rate mechanism without causing too much disruption and without the market believing we have given up our anti-inflationary credentials. And the crisis hit us, and we were toppled out of the exchange rate mechanism before we could reach a conclusion on how to come out voluntarily; and that of course seasoned everything that followed.

HENNESSY

It was almost the end of your Premiership, in that you seriously thought you might have to go, in a sort of honourable resignation, and thereafter you've always been very honest and said you were prone to depression as Prime Minister because of that calamity.

MAJOR

I was never sure whether I should have resigned or not. I asked the views of people I respected, like Douglas Hurd and I think Norman Fowler, and also people who were not politicians, about whether I should resign. And their view, maybe people always give this view, I don't know, but their view was unequivocally that I shouldn't, and that if a Prime Minister did resign a few months after winning an election that the government itself was doomed. Now, whether that was the right decision I have never been certain. I have never been absolutely certain.

HENNESSY

You're still not sure.

MAJOR

I don't think you can ever be certain, and it's not something that haunts me now – but the truth of the matter is I was never certain that it was the right or wrong decision. But it did have several effects. I was never in any doubt that winning the 1997 election would be very difficult. The day after the '92 election, Chris Patten and I sat in the White Room at Number 10 …

HENNESSY

He'd just lost his seat …

MAJOR

Chris had just lost his seat at Bath, and we agreed that in winning a fourth successive term, we had stretched the democratic elastic as far as it would go and, unless Labour collapsed, we would have little chance of winning the next election. I was reinforced in that view by the impact of Black Wednesday. I thought it overwhelmingly likely that we would lose. In once sense, that was liberating: Sarah Hogg, the head of my policy unit, for one repeatedly said to me, you can now do what you think is right, you don't have to politically trim, you can do what you think is right. And economically, we did. And if I may say so, people these days forget the dire economic circumstances on the 30th of November 1990 …

HENNESSY

When you became Prime Minister …

MAJOR

… and the fact that we handed on to the Labour Party in 1997, by common consent, the best economy any government has handed on to its successors, probably at any time in the 20th century. And people forget that. And they forget other things that happened after Black Wednesday: the Northern Ireland peace process, which was extraordinarily difficult to start, but extraordinarily worthwhile.

HENNESSY

I think history will linger on that, because you opened the back-channel to the IRA, after they'd approached MI6 saying the war's over, we need advice on how to finish it. That was an enormous risk, and it was kept very secret as it had to be but it started the road to where we are now.

MAJOR

I remember the afternoon that message came in. I was sitting in Number 10, it was a grizzly, grey late afternoon, and my principal private secretary came in bearing a message, saying, we're not sure what to make of this. And that was the famous message about bringing the conflict to an end. And I discussed it with the Northern Ireland secretary, Patrick Mayhew, and we realised that if this went wrong, it would be the end of our political careers, because we would have been seen as being dupes of the IRA and foolish and naive and all those things. On the other hand, if we made progress it would save people's lives. So that was the judgement: looking foolish on one hand, and perhaps making progress and saving lives on the other. So we were in no doubt about what we should do. But there was a lot of opposition to what we did, both within the Cabinet and in the Conservative Party particularly. I received a lot of support then from the Labour Party and the Liberal party, but I was never sure quite where the balance of opinion was within my own party.

HENNESSY

I'm very struck by Sarah Hogg saying, now you can be yourself; a sense of liberation, as you put it. I've always had the impression though, John, that if you could do it again, you would have been even more yourself. There are certain things you would have done if you'd followed your instincts despite, perhaps, difficulties. One of which would have been to put a lot more funding into the NHS, or another area which you've always been keen on, which is open government. Do you have some regrets that you weren't even more John Major, the inner John Major, than you actually turned out to be '92-'97?

MAJOR

Well, it wasn't just political inhibitions. It was money. I mentioned earlier the terrible economic recession that we had at the beginning of the 1990s: we spent the best part of five to six years putting that right. And it was very unpopular putting that right. And, of course, when you're doing that, you do not have the resources, or in some ways the political capital – with a tiny majority which was shrinking all the time – to actually make those sort of changes. And I couldn't, because we were preoccupied with the economy; we were overwhelmed with disputes about Europe; Northern Ireland also took a great deal of time. But in terms of the social reforms I would like to have made, I'm not sure we would have had the majority for them in the House of Commons. But above all, we didn't have the money for them.

HENNESSY

What would they have been, if I could retrospectively wave a magic wand for you?

MAJOR

Well, I think there are several different areas I would talk about. Firstly, education. Not having had much of it, I'm very much in favour of other people getting it, and widening it. I mean we did, for example, give greater status to the polytechnics – and many people criticised us for this, in some ways maybe they were right.

But I was trying to improve the quality of, the social ambience sur-
rounding, blue-collar work. Certainly a lot of education changes.
I would have liked to have upgraded the education profession. I
think in this mercenary age we would have had to have looked at
the rewards for the top of education. So I think it would have been
expensive to do what I wished to, but I believe it would have been
right to do it. And I think also I would have looked to the provision of more homes, largely small units in the inner cities. And
there's a lot of space, idle space, in and around the cities where I
would have wished to provide, probably, penalties for those who
idly hung on for too long to land that ought to be developed, and
incentives to people actually to develop. And of course, I would
have wanted to make reforms to the health system. Now I believe,
with the money that we had built up in the economy by '97, that we
too, had we won that election, would have put a lot more money
into the health service, and looked at reforms of the health service.
So I shall live with regret to my dying day that I did not have the
wherewithal, and was not in a political position, to go down the
route of those reforms which were the sort of things I wished to do
from the first moment I dreamed of going into politics.

HENNESSY

Another problem which beset your government was the 'back to
basics' idea, which was, I think, misunderstood.

MAJOR

No, it wasn't misunderstood, Peter, it was *distorted*. And it was
distorted because at that stage the government was the fox and
the media were the hounds. In defence of the media, there was,
though I did not know it at the time, a young briefer at central
office who had spoken to people about it being a moral crusade,
when it was never intended to be a moral crusade. If you go back to
the source speech for 'back to basics', it was predominantly about
education and good neighbourliness and community care. And

secondly, for the first three months of it, it was very popular until events conspired to turn it into a negative. But it was distorted.

HENNESSY

Is it possible to have a private life as a modern politician? Because you've suffered very much in that department yourself.

MAJOR

It's increasingly difficult. I admire people who go into politics; I know this isn't fashionable to say at the moment but most of the politicians I know – and I make no party distinction here – the vast majority of the politicians I have known over the years go into politics for good motives, not bad. I don't subscribe to the lurid version of politicians only being in politics for themselves and for their own interests. That was not my experience during the years I was in politics.

HENNESSY

It's a tough, scarring business being Prime Minister, even in relatively benign circumstances, and you didn't have those. I was very struck, years ago now, when Quintin Hailsham was asked on Radio 4 by Anthony Clare, did he regret not becoming Prime Minister when he was so close to it in '63 – the Macmillan succession – and he said: 'I've known every Prime Minister to a greater or lesser extent since Balfour, and most of them have died unhappy; it doesn't lead to happiness'. Are you happy, John? Will you die happy?

MAJOR

Well I very much hope so! I'm not planning to do so immediately; I shall hope to hang on for a while. I think there's different sorts of Prime Ministers once they leave office: there are those for whom office never quite goes away; there are others to a greater extent, and I hope I'm one of them, who have been able to say, that was yesterday, and I now have other things that I must do with the rest of my life. So the advice I would give to anyone who wishes to be Prime Minister is, when it is over, there is a very remarkable world out there. Try and see it, and try and make up for the things you necessarily and rightly had to sacrifice when you were in politics.

HENNESSY

Finally, John, how do you think history will remember you, and how do you want history to remember you? Is there a gap between the two?

MAJOR

[*Laughs*] I have no idea, but the great comfort is, I won't be here to find out.

HENNESSY

[*Laughing*] John Major, thank you very much.

Roy Hattersley (Lord Hattersley)

Series 2, Episode 2, first broadcast 20 August 2014

Born 28 December 1932; **Educated** Sheffield City
Grammar School; University of Hull

MP (Labour) Birmingham, Sparkbrook 1964–97

Joint Parliamentary Secretary, Department of Employment and
Productivity, 1967–69; Minister of Defence for Administration, Ministry
of Defence, 1969–70; Minister of State, Foreign and Commonwealth
Office, 1974–76; Secretary of State for Prices and Consumer
Protection, 1976–79, Deputy Leader of the Labour Party, 1983–92

Autobiography *Who Goes Home?*, 1995

HENNESSY

With me today is Roy Hattersley, a writer and politician, both a
historian of and a participant in events since first elected to the
House of Commons in 1964. In his very person he carries the
history of the Labour Party: from its shining high tide in 1945,
when he was a schoolboy, through the Wilson and Callaghan
governments of the 1960s and 1970s, becoming Deputy Leader as
Labour's internal civil war in the 1980s distracted and exhausted
the party. He has a taste for writing, political ideas, political biography and, I hope, for a dash of autobiographical conversation.
Roy, welcome.

HATTERSLEY

Thank you.

HENNESSY

Can we start with your formative influences? To use an old line, the words 'Labour Party' run through you like a stick of Blackpool rock.

HATTERSLEY

There's no doubt I am an environmental Labour Party member, so to speak. My mother was much more active in Labour than my father; she became the mayor of Sheffield. And I admit, until I was 17 or 18, I knew I was Labour, but I couldn't have told you in more than a couple of sentences why I was Labour. Then came the great, dare I use the word, intellectual influence of my life: I was in the lower-sixth, going into upper-sixth; the schoolmaster who was encouraging me gave me some summer reading. It had three books as I recall: Eileen Power's *Medieval People*, Kitto's *The Greeks*, and R. H. Tawney's *Equality*. And I read *Equality*, and it was as if I'd been struck by a thunderbolt. It seemed to me that the case for equality was overwhelming, there was no argument against it. I couldn't understand why people didn't accept it as an obvious matter of fact – and I feel just like that today. *Equality* seems to me to be the good life, the good society, the good nation. And I've felt like that ever since I was 17.

HENNESSY

What year was this Tawney moment?

HATTERSLEY

It would have been 1950, '51.

HENNESSY

'51. And you're at Sheffield Grammar School.

HATTERSLEY

Sheffield Grammar School. But another thing happened shortly afterwards, the following summer. I was working in a vac job on the milk round, naturally enough the Co-operative milk round, Brightside and Carbrook Co-operative Society – there's a title to conjure with. We were delivering milk to everyone who had a milk token. And one Friday morning we got to a house where a woman with two little children said, 'Sorry, no token'. And the real milkman – I was the assistant – said, 'Don't worry love', took out a bottle, said, 'Get a jug', carefully took off the sealed silver foil from the top and poured the milk into the jug, then put the foil back on, smashed the bottle, and said, 'We'll put this down as a smashed'. And I was rather impressed by the way he helped her – this is what society should be about. Two rows later, a woman comes out and says, 'I've no token.' He says, 'Sorry, can't do anything.' I said to him afterwards, 'What was the difference between woman one and woman two?' 'Didn't you notice?', he said, 'The second woman smokes. If she can afford cigarettes, she can afford milk.' And this began in my mind, and set in my heart, a dilemma which I still struggle with: whether benefits, welfare, should be a matter of need, or a matter of earning.

HENNESSY

The deserving poor and the undeserving poor. Very 19th century.

HATTERSLEY

Exactly. And I'm instinctively – I won't say on the side of the undeserving poor, but I see we have to somehow help the undeserving poor. When I hear Duncan Smith talking about people 'deserving benefits', or 'earning it', I have a vision of this archetypal layabout, the man in the singlet sitting in front of a television, watching racing and drinking beer out of a can, and won't go to work. Would we deny him benefits? Well, he's got a downtrodden wife and two neglected children, I mean, you've got to do something with those people despite their lack of 'desert'. And I don't know how you solve that problem, but I've thought about it every day since delivering milk for Brightside and Carbrook.

HENNESSY

You're a classic incarnation of '45 – you're a man of '45, Roy, aren't you?

HATTERSLEY

Well, Robin Day said this. He said, 'Mr Hattersley, wouldn't you have been more at home in Mr Attlee's government than in Mr Callaghan's?' And I said, 'No, Sir Robin, I'd have been more at home in Mr Gladstone's government.' And I think to a certain extent that's true, but I think that '45 was a shining hour of British politics. This is a time when by any standards we had a great government who changed the weather: nothing has been quite the same since '45. And therefore I'm very proud that I once delivered leaflets for the '45 election.

HENNESSY

Now, Gladstone's interesting, because Mrs Thatcher and her people would always quote Mr Gladstone as being the model: free trade, competition …

HATTERSLEY

Sovereigns fructifying in the pockets of the people.

HENNESSY

Exactly. Now, your bit of Mr Gladstone is a different bit of Mr Gladstone to Mrs Thatcher's, I would imagine.

HATTERSLEY

Well, my bit of Mr Gladstone is not his politics, but his character. I have hanging in my house in Derbyshire a cartoon from *Punch* with a slogan underneath, 'Had he been a worse man, he would have been a better politician.' And what better could have been said about anybody than that? He was a man of impeccable integrity, enormous belief, certainty, courage, determination. Much of what he did, apart from Ireland, I disapprove of; but nevertheless he had this strange courage, strength and integrity, which I find immensely attractive.

HENNESSY

Mr Gladstone was a great man, obviously – but he lacked a raucousness gland. You are a very jolly person compared to Mr Gladstone. Mr Gladstone was very thin on jokes, Roy – you rather like jokes.

HATTERSLEY

[*Laughing*] Everybody's a jolly person compared to Mr Gladstone! And he hated jokes, he was very annoyed when people made jokes in his Cabinet, or made jokes to him.

HENNESSY

I have an image in my mind, of the young Roy, January '47, vesting day of the National Coal Board, and you got on your bike if I remember, and you cycled out to the nearest pit to see the notice board going up.

HATTERSLEY

'This pit is managed on behalf of the people by the National Coal Board', or 'This colliery is managed on behalf ... *managed on behalf of the people*'. I mean, what a wonderful phrase.

HENNESSY

And you absorbed all of that.

HATTERSLEY

I absorbed all of it.

HENNESSY

And you're still a public-ownership man with qualifications, aren't you?

HATTERSLEY

Well, I was regarded as a right-wing so-and-so in the Labour Party, because I always argued against nationalising everything, and I've never thought that socialism was about public ownership. But sometimes public ownership is necessary. But public ownership is a means to an end – it's not what socialism is about. Socialism is about equality – and sometimes, to get a more equal society, something has to be publicly owned, but by and large most of the economy has to be run on the market principle. The market principle is essential for freedom as well as for efficiency. But there are some areas where public ownership is the right answer.

HENNESSY

Can we turn now to another great influence on you? The man concerned, who you actually knew – I don't think you knew Tawney – was Tony Crosland, and his *Future of Socialism* in 1956. Now, Crosland's notions of equality are very Tawney-like in many ways, but there's also a raffishness about Tony Crosland – there's that extraordinary sentence in the book, 'We need not only higher exports and old-age pensions, but more open-air cafes, brighter and gayer streets at night, later closing for public houses'. Now, you knew him very well – he's reacting against his Puritan upbringing.

HATTERSLEY

There's a classic completion of the paragraph, which says, 'If socialism is a matter of total abstinence and a good filing cabinet, some of us will fall by the wayside.' And that, in a sense, is what made the book catch on. People wanted socialism to be less grey, less drab, less austere. Tony was, notwithstanding that, a very, very serious politician. He also had more élan than any other politician I have ever known. I was at a Cabinet meeting, before I was in the Cabinet – they must have been discussing something about Europe – it began with Harold Wilson saying, 'There've been too many leaks from this Cabinet, and it's got to stop. It does the party damage, it does the government damage, it does the entire country damage, and I tell you now, it's got to stop.' A long pause – and Tony Crosland said, 'Harold, you only cause us embarrassment by behaving in this way, because we all know 90% of the leaks come from you.' I don't know any other Cabinet minister who would have done that. The Cabinet were stunned. Harold said, 'Let's go on to foreign affairs.' [*Laughter*] And that was the essential, iconoclastic, daring, full-of-élan Tony Crosland, which I found immensely attractive. Very un-Gladstonian, I might say.

HENNESSY

Deeply, deeply! Mr G would have deeply disapproved of T Crosland, absolutely. Tony Crosland had a great friend, Michael Young, who wrote *The Rise of the Meritocracy*, which was a book we all read. They thought about equality of opportunity, IQ + effort = merit, that classic formulation and I remember reading it as a grammar-school boy and thinking, 'What's wrong with this? This is a charter for me.' I didn't realise for a long time it was a satire. You no doubt would have realised it was a satire, and a warning, and you've always had a sense of the ambivalence of meritocracy, even though you were a classic meritocrat.

HATTERSLEY

I don't know what your background was, Peter, but I suspect it was like mine: ideal. If they wanted to form an individual who was the perfect candidate for passing the 11-plus, it would have been me:

my background, my family, my mother's aspirations, my father's attitudes, I was tailor-made to pass the 11-plus.

HENNESSY

Snap.

HATTERSLEY

But it wasn't enough – there are some other people to worry about besides you and me! And that was my basic feeling. But Tony's attempts to define what sort of equality he wanted was a great step forward. Tony clearly doesn't believe in equality of outcome, but he defines the equality he wants in a way that is totally sophisticated: namely, that people are always different, and we don't want to smother the differences. You are cleverer than somebody else, tougher than somebody else, more feeble – those are personal differences which can't be overcome, we don't want to overcome them. But we want to eliminate those differences that are imposed on us by society rather than by nature. And that's what Tony called 'democratic equality'.

HENNESSY

And that explains, does it, for all your fondness of your own schooling, that you've been a comprehensive-school advocate right through.

HATTERSLEY

Right through. I put myself back by at least five years when I was Education Spokesman, when against the wishes of Harold Wilson – I didn't know it was against his wishes – but I made a speech to the independent schools telling them that if I had my way I'd abolish them. Because I made the speech, I didn't become Education Spokesman after '74. I'd done two hard years shadowing Mrs Thatcher, and I assumed that when the election was over and won I would do the Education job; but not only did I not do the

Education job, I got no job at all for three weeks. I was left hanging about for three weeks to punish me for various sins!

HENNESSY

I've always felt very strongly that the one ministerial job you craved above all others – perhaps it would have been nice to be Prime Minister – but above all you wanted to be Education Secretary.

HATTERSLEY

Yes. I always did. The last time it was remotely possible was when John Smith was leader of the Labour Party, and he wanted me to stay on and be in his Cabinet. We were great friends, John Smith and me. And he had this view, 'Won't you stay on and see us in?' Which I assumed meant that I did one of these non-departmental jobs until they knew where to hang the coats and where the lavatories were in 10 Downing Street and then I was summarily ejected; I didn't want to do that. And when I went to see him, five days before he died, to tell him I was announcing my retirement the next day, he said, 'I would like you in the Cabinet.' I said, 'No. On no terms.' He said, 'Well, what if I offered you Education?' And I paused. He said, 'I'm not going to, so don't worry about it.' [*Laughs*] But right until then, Education was still in my mind, in my heart.

HENNESSY

If I could retrospectively wave a wand and give you the Education Department, tell me what you would have done; what would have been the sequence of actions, and what would have been the cumulative effect you would have sought?

HATTERSLEY

I wanted secondary education in particular to be unsegregated. We want all secondary schools to be similar in funding, if possible in esteem, and therefore in outcome. We want a unity in the secondary schools, rather than the divisions into various categories of acceptability and unacceptability. That means accepting that some parents will behave rather better than other parents. When you say parents with sharp elbows and determined characters push their children into certain schools, you're said to be denouncing the parents at the bottom end of the scale who don't bother doing that. Well, you may be, but it's a fact. Some parents push their children, some don't, and you don't want the education system to allow that to happen and to accentuate it.

HENNESSY

In effect, Roy, what you would have been seeking to do was to syringe out the class and status obsessions of our dear country from the education world.

HATTERSLEY

Well, as footballers say, that's a big ask. [*Laughs*] But I would like to nibble at the class system in this country. If I'd been able to just nibble away a tiny bit at the edges of it, I would die happy.

HENNESSY

Was Tony Crosland your route to Hugh Gaitskell?

HATTERSLEY

No, I was always a Gaitskellite before those days. I was always on what was called the moderate wing of the Labour Party. And I became devoted to Gaitskell's's cause during the nuclear disarmament crisis.

HENNESSY

1960, '59-'60.

HATTERSLEY

At that time I almost gave up looking for a Parliamentary seat. I was turned down for a very large number of Parliamentary seats;

it was becoming rather a wearisome business, going around the country and not being selected. And I thought I probably didn't want to do it. I was a big noise on the Sheffield council, I was chairman of the Housing Committee when I was 25; I guess I would have been leader of the council if I'd stayed on. And then I went to a party conference, and there was a great argument over nuclear disarmament, and Hugh Gaitskell I suppose touched my emotions, by promising to fight, fight, and fight again to save the party we love. And I wanted to be a footsoldier in the battle. So I went home and said to the regional organiser in Yorkshire and said, 'I'm still in the race. If you can find a seat I can look for, I'll still go for it.'

HENNESSY

Did you think, Roy, in '64, even though Labour came back with a very small majority of three or four, depending on how you count, that '64 could be another shining hour, it could be '45 again?

HATTERSLEY

No I didn't. I thought that the next election might be; I thought that Harold Wilson was quite right to form a government and then go to the country for a second term quite soon. But in some ways, it *was* a shining hour you know: social policy was wonderful in '66. And when you think about what we did about social policy and libertarianism, Roy Jenkins' first period as Home Secretary, all that was immensely important. We made some bad mistakes over the economy, and we made a bad mistake on the first day by not devaluing – if we'd devalued, then we'd have had the economy moving forward in the way we needed to. But as a social government, as a reforming government in terms of individual liberty, it was a very, very important government.

HENNESSY

It's interesting you talk about the devaluation, because it's almost a conventional wisdom that it choked off all sorts of possibilities, that inflated exchange rate, it was far too high, it was not reduced until 1967. But the other aspect of you which I've noticed over the years was that if you couldn't have Education, you wanted to run a Ministry of Production, and you had developed ideas about what a production, a DTI, whatever you want to call it, a Board of Trade transformed would be. And yet there was the Department of Economic Affairs, and growth was the idea, indicative planning, a British version of the French planning system – and yet it didn't work, Roy, the growth rate stayed stubbornly where it had always been, with endless balance of payment crises.

HATTERSLEY

Well, I think it's all down to that basic first decision, and the first mistake. Jim Callaghan, to whom I was very close in the end, he put me in his Cabinet, Jim said to me perfectly openly when I discussed this with him, that the reason for doing it was political rather than economic. They didn't want the reputation that the Labour Party comes in and always devalues. It had devalued twice before, if it devalued a third time …

HENNESSY

'31 and '49.

HATTERSLEY

Yes. The reason was entirely political that they didn't. And Jim I think in the end regretted that they didn't.

HENNESSY

Yes. Looking back to those Wilson years, though – it was the social-democratic hour in many ways, not just those social-libertarian reforms that you've already referred to, but there was Wilson's rhetoric about technology and the scientific race, and where the future of world economic competition would be decided, and all the rest of it. Although people diminish it now, that 'White

Heat of Technology' speech he gave at the Scarborough Conference in '63, and the first attempts to do planning based on that, to take it a step on beyond the Attlee government, were all very promising, and many of us fell for it completely as young men. I certainly did.

HATTERSLEY

Well, I fell for it, and I was still falling for it when I was in my 40s in the Cabinet. And had we won the election, I would have had that beefed-up department, with things taken off from the Treasury.

HENNESSY

If you'd won in '79?

HATTERSLEY

If we'd won in '79. Jim told me, at the last press conference at Transport House, on the Monday, that when we won he was going to divide the Treasury into two parts, David Owen was going to get one part of it, I was going to get another part, and mine was basically going to be the Ministry of Industry. And he said, 'Which part would you like?' and I rather annoyed him in saying, 'The part that's called Chancellor of the Exchequer'. [*Hennessy laughs*] Which he thought was being flippant about serious things. But anyway I would have wanted it, because I still believe in what you call indicative planning. I don't believe governments tell industry what to do, but you've got to ask industry what they want doing, and do it to the best of your ability. And very often governments don't do what industry wants, they do something that they believe to be right when it isn't.

HENNESSY

Before '79 you had this tremendous crisis, the sterling crisis of '76, which I think you've always thought was overdone because the Treasury forecasts were misleading, I think that's been your case.

But you were with Tony Crosland in the Cabinet, not where Jim Callaghan and Denis Healey wanted you to be.

HATTERSLEY

I was the other boy on the bridge, there weren't three men on the bridge, there were only two. And we were right, but we were wrong. Our economics were right; Tony Crosland was prepared to gamble – I had no capability of working out the figures – that the public-sector borrowing requirement was not as large as the Treasury said – nor was it. In fact, we probably weren't in deficit at all. We argued as best we could that there should be a less austere view of public expenditure, and that to attack it in the way we eventually did attack it would undermine the Labour Party, and the idea of public expenditure for ever, as it did. But we were wrong in that we underestimated the importance of keeping world opinion on our side. I remember Professor Maurice Peston, now Lord Peston, who was then my special adviser, saying to me, 'The Prime Minister and Healey are totally wrong, but you have to support them. You have to support them because international opinion won't allow you to do anything else. If the Prime Minister says that international opinion requires the Cabinet to jump off Westminster Bridge, then the Cabinet must jump off Westminster Bridge. The merits don't matter, it's just getting international opinion on our side.' And I remember sitting in my room the night before the ultimate Cabinet meeting -

HENNESSY

This is December 1976 ...

HATTERSLEY

That's right. And Tony had been on some foreign jaunt, he was Foreign Secretary then, with Jim, and he came into my room and he said, 'It's all up,' and I said, 'What do you mean?' and he said, 'Well, the Prime Minister wants us to support him, and I knew that when he came to me and said, "You've got to support me, otherwise we're in trouble," I'd have to say "Yes". You must do the same'. And I said, 'Of course I will.' So the next day we had a very, very mild Cabinet, and we all agreed to everything.

HENNESSY

Then Labour's civil war began, not that visibly straight away, but in '79, with the Winter of Discontent. It must have been very painful for you, Roy, because the Party of '45, that coalition of the wider Labour movement and so on began to fragment, and the malice, the sheer detestation of certain bits of the party, already talking about betrayal, started even before you'd lost the election of '79.

HATTERSLEY

Much more painful than the divisions was the destruction of the idea. I mean, my social democracy, or Labour Party enthusiasm had as part of its bedrock the fact that the trade unions were a force for good, and that public expenditure was essential for a civilised society. Within the space of a year, we'd seen the trade unions behave hideously, and we'd seen public expenditure unsustainable. And to see those two pillars kicked away was very, very damaging, and I don't think the Labour Party's recovered from it even now.

HENNESSY

And then after the election loss, the Party turned in on itself and the electoral college was changed to reduce the Parliamentary Labour Party's say; and there was a whole succession of set-backs for you and your colleagues that in effect, took away the '80s from you. It should have been your salad days, to use an old phrase, you would have had one of the highest offices in the land, if Labour had formed a government at any time in the '80s; but it was all taken away from you as the Party fragmented.

HATTERSLEY

Well, we came out of the '79 last Cabinet meeting – we being the members of Cabinet of about 40, Bill Rodgers, Shirley Williams, John Smith – and we all said, well, we may have to wait five years, or perhaps 10 years, but we'll all still be 50. We all believed we'd be back soon despite all the ructions. We did lose those years – but they weren't fruitless years. In a strange, paradoxical way what made the years tolerable was having something else important to do and that important thing to do was getting the Labour Party right. I think I would have found it much more difficult just sitting there waiting for the next election, than I felt trying to help Neil as best I could to get the Labour Party back on its feet again. That gave us a purpose; it was a different purpose, but it was a purpose.

HENNESSY

There was a fascinating emotional geography between you and Neil Kinnock, because you're very different in many ways, but I think you had that shared Tawney-ism, you had that equality impulse, and in many ways you weren't the odd couple people expected you to be.

HATTERSLEY

Neil wouldn't mind me saying that in some ways we were chalk and cheese. But in fact I knew Neil Kinnock was the right man for the job, and that in fact helped, the fact that I knew Neil would be able to get the Labour Party right in a way that I wouldn't have been able to do.

HENNESSY

You got on very well with John Smith, you were flesh of each other's flesh ideologically, weren't you, as well as good friends. He was the leader that was taken away in tragic circumstances. One of the New Labour arguments that one heard in 1997 quite a lot, although not in public, was that 'John wouldn't have got us a big majority'. Some people even thought he wouldn't have won in '97.

HATTERSLEY

Well, there's no question he would have won. He wouldn't have won it with as big a majority as Tony, because he wouldn't have appealed to those middle-class people who thought, 'Say what you like about Blair, he's not a socialist.' They wouldn't have said that about John. But he would have been sufficiently stable a Prime Minister to do the things he needed to do. And I think life would have been very different; we'd have had a proper Labour government, and life would have been very different indeed.

HENNESSY

It's interesting you use the words 'proper Labour government' – in what way were Tony Blair's successive governments improper?

HATTERSLEY

Well, let's put it this way: when I complain bitterly over the commercialisation of the Health Service, the Conservative Party say, 'But you began it'. When I complain bitterly that we're not building enough houses, they say, 'But you didn't build any houses.' When I say, 'You rely too much on the market, light-touch regulations,' they say, 'But you were the originators of light-touch regulations.' The things we started we enabled the new Tories to take on, and I think that is a very, very severe criticism.

HENNESSY

Did you feel that Tony Blair travelled light intellectually? That he wasn't rooted in the Labour Party in terms of loving it in the way you did, but also cerebrally ...

HATTERSLEY

The two things are different. He was a very clever man. He worked for me; his first job was when I was shadow chancellor, and he was the lad who did the running about late at night. And he was marvellous: he was lucid, he was loyal, he was hard-working, and he was very clever. But he came to politics very late: at university he wasn't really interested in politics, if at all. And therefore many books that you and I had read when we were in our teens he'd never heard of. For instance, he'd never heard of *The Rise of the Meritocracy*. And I think therefore that he snatched hold of some half-thought-out ideas, like the market, and hung on to them, without having thought about it quite so clearly as he should have done. I think that was one of his problems, that he didn't have the roots in the movement, and in the economic background to politics in general.

HENNESSY

Now, you're an ace political biographer: if you were writing Gordon Brown's political biography, that still would be a mystery to you, would it? Why he turned out the way he did in the Premiership?

HATTERSLEY

I have to say, because the requirement of honesty pervades the programme, I fear it was personality problems, it wasn't political problems, it was personality. I think he waited too long – the sort of Prince of Wales effect, the worst kings we've had have all been Princes of Wales who waited too long.

HENNESSY

That's a bit disloyal, Roy.

HATTERSLEY

Well, he's not King yet. [*Laughs*] I'm not anticipating he'll be as bad as George IV. [*Laughs*] I won't go any further in case you cut it out of the programme.

HENNESSY

Did your friendships with Shirley Williams and David Owen and Bill Rodgers recover? The others of the Gang of Four? Because you're of the same generation – you and Shirley in particular were very close operators together. Great friends.

HATTERSLEY

Great friends. We went on family holiday together. And my relationship with Shirley Williams survived the Gang of Four more easily than it will survive her support for the present Health Bill, which I find very difficult to swallow.

HENNESSY

She did a lot to modify that, to be fair.

HATTERSLEY

She did very little to modify it.

HENNESSY

Ah.

HATTERSLEY

She claims she did a lot to modify it, but if you look at the differences, the differences are *all* superficial.

HENNESSY

She would dispute that, wouldn't she?

HATTERSLEY

Well, I'm sure she would. The friendship with Bill was always an acquaintanceship rather, but with no animosity. And David and I, now we're friends again, we've recovered from it all.

HENNESSY

Friendship matters to you in politics, doesn't it, Roy? You've never been a loner.

HATTERSLEY

I'm not sure. I've never wanted to move in a clique, I've never wanted to join things. I mean, I've never been on a Parliamentary excursion abroad anywhere, I've never done those communal things that politicians do. When I stood for the leadership, one of the things that was held against me was that I was never about in the Tea Room and the Dining Room, but I'm not that sort of politician.

HENNESSY

The next book …

HATTERSLEY

The working title is *The Catholics*. But it's not a theological work, which I'm hardly equipped to write! It's a history of how Catholicism survived. My last book was the story of the Cavendish family, *The Devonshires*, and having written 250,000 words, it suddenly struck me that they spent very many years of their lives, over five or six centuries, suppressing Catholicism. It struck me, given that oppression that had gone on for 600 years, that it's a miracle, perhaps in my sense rather than the Catholic sense, that it had survived so long. And that's what I'm writing about.

HENNESSY

Has it anything to do with your dad as well, who was a Catholic priest as a young man?

HATTERSLEY

The dedication will be, 'To Father Roy Hattersley, born such a date, died such a date, ordained such a date, excommunicated such a date.' But that's only vaguely the reason. I didn't know my father was a priest until after he died.

HENNESSY

How did you feel when your mum told you about all of that?

HATTERSLEY

I felt desperately sorry I didn't know beforehand. Because I loved my father deeply; perhaps that's obvious to say, people do. But I loved him in a different way from the way I loved my mother. My mother was a very tough, demanding woman, a very hard woman in many ways; my father was very soft, gentle, yielding sort of man, and I could write down all sorts of virtues he possessed. But the idea that he committed this great act of bravery – that he walked away from the Church for love. I would have like to have known that he had a heroic moment while he was alive, and I think it was a heroic moment. I would have liked to have been able to say to my dad, 'I'm very proud of you for doing that.'

HENNESSY

You can say that in the book.

HATTERSLEY

I shall, believe me, I shall. [*Hennessy laughs*]

HENNESSY

Roy, what trace do you think you'll leave on political history?

HATTERSLEY

Very little.

HENNESSY

Why?

HATTERSLEY

Well, I've been a middle-ranking politician, I've never had one of the great offices of state. I think since you invite me to be self-congratulatory that I did something to save the Labour Party in the bad years. Before we had really begun the revival I set up a really rather ludicrous organisation called the Solidarity Campaign, which had only one purpose, which was to demonstrate to people in the country there were still reasonable people in the Labour Party. The Labour Party wasn't divided between the extremists who'd left to do absurd things or who demanded absurd things, and the moderates who'd left to be moderate. There was a core, a little flickering light of common sense and social democracy in the Labour Party. And we set it up to create that impression, and we did create that truthful impression. And I think that had I not imparted that, had we not had that idea of the continuity of Attlee socialism, as you like to call it, I think the Labour Party would have been in terrible trouble. So when I get to the pearly gates, and they say, 'Why should you come in?' I'll say, 'Because I helped to save the Labour Party in the 1970s.'

HENNESSY

What trace would you have liked to have left, if I could wave that magic wand again?

HATTERSLEY

I think I would like to have made great social changes, I would like to have changed the structure of British education; I would like to have made it a genuinely egalitarian operation. Of course, I would have liked to have been Prime Minister, everyone who gets into Cabinet would like to be Prime Minister – but I don't think I would have been a very dramatic or historically important Prime Minister. I wouldn't have wanted to do great things; I would have just wanted to make Britain a more equal society, a more compassionate society, a more amenable society.

HENNESSY

Roy, thank you very much.

HATTERSLEY

It's been a pleasure.

David Steel (Lord Steel of Aikwood)

Series 2, Episode 3, first broadcast 27 August 2014

Born 31 March 1938; **Educated** Prince of Wales School, Nairobi; George Watson's College, Edinburgh; Edinburgh University.

MP (Liberal) Roxburgh, Selkirk and Peebles (1965–83); Tweeddale, Ettrick and Lauderdale 1983–97 (as a Liberal Democrat 1988–97).

Leader of the Liberal Party, 1976–88; Co-founder, Social and Liberal Democrats, 1988.

Autobiography *Against Goliath,* 1989

HENNESSY

David Steel has been a real presence in our national political conversation for nearly 50 years, since he became a Liberal MP in 1965 at the age of 26. He quickly left an enduring mark by piloting the 1967 Abortion Act through the House of Commons, which to this day leaves him reviled and praised by those who feel passionate about the practice. Now 76, he retains a youthful air, and occasionally he is still referred to as 'the boy David'. He's been a key and sustained player in the shift from two-party politics to a multi-party system. David, welcome.

STEEL

Thank you.

HENNESSY

You were born in 1938 in Kirkcaldy, the son of a Presbyterian minister in the Church of Scotland. Do you think deep down, or perhaps not so deep, you're still a son of the manse?

STEEL

Oh yes, I think it never leaves you; ask Gordon Brown. [*Laughs*] I think it's just there. My father was very much involved in promoting better conditions for the miners on the Fife coalfields, in particular showers at the mines, so they didn't go home to sit in a tin bath in front of the fire. So that sort of influence was there.

HENNESSY

Did it make you perhaps a tad preachy as well, do you think?

STEEL

Preachy in a good sense, yes. Because I had to listen to my father's sermons twice on a Sunday, I was aware that speeches should have a structure, a beginning, a theme and an end. And I have to say, many of the speeches of political leaders today have no structure whatsoever, they're just a series of unconnected sound-bites. [*Laughs*] So, certainly my speeches at the party conferences, which were always the big annual event, had an awful lot of preparation put in them, and were very much structured along the lines of a sermon.

HENNESSY

When you were 11, your father was appointed to a ministry in what was still called 'Keenya', now Kenya, and suddenly you were uprooted from Scotland to Africa, and I know the Mau Mau emergency didn't erupt until a few years later, but again it must have been an extraordinary formation, utterly different from the one you'd experienced in Scotland.

STEEL

It was in fact that four years that I spent in Kenya which were the most formative influence in my life, it's how I became a Liberal. It was international affairs that brought me into politics. My background of my having been brought up in Kenya – including the tail-end, when the Mau Mau rebellion was just starting – affected me because when I went to university at the time of the Sharpeville Massacre in South Africa, the Conservative government was still trying to inflict the Central African Federation on Rhodesia and Nyasaland … these were the formative influences that caused me to be interested in party politics.

HENNESSY

Being in favour of colonial freedom, as it were, across the piece in Africa, could have made you a Labour Party person just as easily. Why did it take the Liberal form rather than the Labour form?

STEEL

You're quite right. Someone who became a great friend of mine later on was John P. Mackintosh, who you will remember was the Labour MP in the next-door constituency, but before that he was actually one of my lecturers when I was a student. And he tried to get me to join the Labour Party. He took me to a meeting which Hugh Gaitskell addressed and I was very impressed. And I won't say I was teetering on the brink of joining the Labour Party, but what stopped me was that the next day Hugh Gaitskell was howled down by his own party in Glasgow at a speech, and I thought, 'Do I really want to be involved in a party that spends all its time fighting its leader?' Actually, I knew that I wasn't a socialist, but it seemed to me, by process of elimination I joined the Liberal Club at Edinburgh University.

HENNESSY

It's to your credit: there's no trace of careerism in that decision because at that time, I think, the Liberal Party had six MPs, and it used to be unkindly said that the entire Liberal Parliamentary Party could have its weekly meeting in a taxi.

STEEL

I wasn't thinking about a political career at all. I mean, I was studying law at Edinburgh, but I had an interest in politics, and I had an interest in debating, and I took part in union debates, including debates against people from Glasgow like John Smith and Donald Dewar – it was that sort of era.

HENNESSY

So what turned you towards the idea of perhaps pursuing a political career?

STEEL

I was president of the Student Representative Council, which two years later was a sabbatical post, but at my time it wasn't, so I was spending all my time running student affairs and so on, and doing very little legal work. And when I completed my degree I'd decided by that time that I didn't want to be a lawyer anyway, and I didn't quite know what I wanted to do, and the Liberal Party offered me a job, as Assistant Secretary in the office in Scotland. It was supposed to be a year, but because Alec Douglas-Home put off the election, it turned out to be two years. And that's actually what led me into a political career.

HENNESSY

And you stood for Roxburgh, Selkirk and Peebles, in the October '64 election.

STEEL

Well, that in itself was another unexpected event. It was a seat where we had always been in second place, and we had no candidate. And I was going to fight a seat in Edinburgh where the main objective was to save my deposit. And I remember Jo Grimond coming into the office and saying, 'That seat has got to be fought' – in those days the Liberal Party didn't fight all its seats. 'But we cannot have a seat where we've been in second place and not fight it. And so, young Steel, if nobody else will do it, you'll have to go and do it.' And so I did. And then, six weeks after the election, the sitting MP, who was only 63, died totally unexpectedly. So there was a by-election, and I won it. So, you couldn't have planned that, Peter, it just happened. [*Laughs*]

HENNESSY

Like all the good things.

STEEL

I always say that, you know, that people like you write political textbooks, but the one word which is very important, which doesn't appear anywhere in any of your books, is the word 'luck'.

HENNESSY

It will from now on.

STEEL

[*Laughs*] Thank you!

HENNESSY

Can you remember the shock of Westminster? What was it like, in terms of what you expected it to be and what you didn't expect it to be?

STEEL

Well, it was quite a shock because, living in Scotland, I think I'd only ever been to the House of Commons once. It was also a shock being the youngest member. I was called 'the boy David', something which I hated at the time – I quite like it now! [*laughs*] – but in those days it was a bit off-putting. And intimidating, really.

HENNESSY

Can you remember who coined it first?

STEEL

It was John Bannerman, I think, who was the chairman of the Scottish Liberal Party, but it was taken up by the *Daily Express*, and in fact, when I won they had a special edition printed, and the front page headline was, 'It's Boy David!'

HENNESSY

How come you took up the very sensitive and delicate and controversial question of abortion when you came top, or very near the top, of the backbenchers' ballot for private-members' bills?

STEEL

Yes, I was number three in the ballot, and what had happened was that the Abortion Law Reform Association had lobbied all the candidates in the '64 election with a questionnaire and a leaflet, saying, 'If elected, will you support reform of the abortion law?' And I read this stuff, I didn't know much about the subject, and I ticked the box saying 'Yes, if elected, I will support it.' Vera Houghton, who was the wife of Douglas Houghton, then Chairman of the Labour Party, was hanging around in the corridors outside, waiting to see who'd won a place in the ballot. And she knew which MPs had ticked this box, so she made a beeline for me and said, would I consider doing this, and I decided to take that on. Again, luck played a part, because if you remember it was a very long parliament that one, it began in March after the second Wilson election of '66, and if we hadn't had the full 18 months instead of a year, I don't think it would have got through.

HENNESSY

Did you have any feeling in the late '60s, as you settled down into parliament and became quite a big figure, quite quickly, that the Liberals might just, in your lifetime, have a chance of a whiff of power, if not alone, then in combination with the Labour Party?

STEEL

I think I always assumed that on the way to the possible reappearance of a Liberal government there would have to be some kind of coalition, or partnership. It did occur to me that there would have to be a way through to government which would involve partnership with another party, and I have to say at that time I was thinking all the time of the Labour Party.

HENNESSY

In February '74 the prospect more than flickered of some kind of arrangement in coalition, or some kind of deal, when the Liberals won 20% of the vote in the first of the elections, in February '74, and Ted Heath called in Jeremy Thorpe, the Liberal leader, for that long weekend to try and do a deal with him. Were you tempted to tell Jeremy Thorpe, 'We should go for this'?

STEEL

Not in the least. And in fact, it was very fleeting. I mean, a lot of people have written about that period as though it was a serious proposition. It never really was. I actually drove Jeremy Thorpe on the second occasion to go and see Ted Heath, and lurked in the car park outside. The election results were coming in on the Friday. By Monday the idea was dead. It was never a possibility, and in fact on the Sunday, Jo Grimond, myself and Frank Byers, who was the elder statesman of the party, leader of the party in Lords, had already met, and told Jeremy this was just not on. And it was not on for three reasons. One was that Liberals plus Tories did not form a majority; two, we'd be propping up a Prime Minister who'd gone to the country voluntarily seeking a mandate and lost; and thirdly, we couldn't really be associated with the Conservatives. So, it was never really a serious proposition, certainly not in my mind. In fact, one of the reasons I hastened down to London was to make sure it didn't happen. [*Laughs*]

HENNESSY

Did you suspect that Jeremy Thorpe was rather tempted, that he'd been offered the Home Office? Temptation might have been too much?

STEEL

I think he was a bit tempted by it. I mean, who wouldn't be? If you've been leader of the party and suddenly a place in Cabinet is being dangled before you – you might have some fleeting temptation. But by the time we met on the Monday, the four of us, he had realised it was not going to happen. And when the MPs met, if I remember rightly, on the Monday evening it was completely killed off. The MPs all agreed, and said that this was not on; we're not going to have a coalition. We had to continue the meeting because the press were hanging around outside and it didn't look very good if we all finished it in 20 minutes flat. And what I do remember about that meeting, very firmly, was Jo Grimond saying, 'Look, the decision we've made is the right one, but some of the things some of you have been saying are completely wrong. If we're a party that believes in proportional representation, and if we hope to advance towards government, then at some stage the thought of coalition has got to enter our minds. And it's no good saying that in principle you're opposed to a coalition. So he was taking some of his colleagues to task for having a fundamentalist view against having a coalition ever. And I always remembered that, and I remembered it when the opportunity came up of doing a deal with Jim Callaghan, which was a very different proposition because it was more than midway through a Parliament, and it was in the face of a no-confidence motion which Mrs Thatcher put down.

HENNESSY

And Labour, for you, given your social-democratic leanings, would be the natural coalition or pact partner?

STEEL

Yes. At the time they were trying to put through the devolution proposals – not very successfully – but we managed in the course of the Lib-Lab Pact to re-jig the whole of the legislation. They were keen on an incomes policy, which we were as well at that time. They were willing to have co-ordination on policy, help for small businesses, a little bit of industrial partnership and so on. So it seemed to me to have all the makings of a reasonable agreement, not a coalition, but just an agreement to sustain the government so that it would have the parliamentary majority and the confidence to deal with the financial situation.

HENNESSY

Personalities matter terribly in these arrangements. You and Jim – he was Uncle Jim to you really, I mean he thought the world of you.

STEEL

But he was that kind of character, wasn't he? I mean, he was the nation's Uncle Jim; he wasn't just my Uncle Jim. He was a very avuncular figure. I don't think we had any rows during the whole of that 18-month period. And in fact I remember when we finally ended the agreement and said, 'Look, you know, you really ought to be having an election', he said – which was very strange – he said, 'Oh, I really would like to have you in my Cabinet'. And then later, when he made the mistake of not going to the country in the autumn, I said to him years afterwards, 'Well, why didn't you?' and he said to me, 'Well, I couldn't be assured of a majority.' And I said, 'What was wrong with that? We were doing quite nicely.' So there seemed to be a contradiction between what he said to me in a private meeting at the time, and his public attitude later.

HENNESSY

I think he told me once that he'd thought of you in his own Cabinet; he was very keen if he'd won in '79 that you should be in the Cabinet. Did you actually talk about what job you might have done? How far did that conversation go?

STEEL

No, not at all. The conversation was not pursued in any way, no.

HENNESSY

Would you have been tempted? Do you rather regret it didn't come about?

STEEL

Oh, I think if he'd gone in the autumn and there'd been a hung Parliament we would certainly have formed a coalition then, yes. Yes, it could have been very different.

HENNESSY

And no Mrs Thatcher, no 1980s.

STEEL

Mrs Thatcher would have been deferred even more. She never forgave me for deferring her coming to power anyway. [*Laughs*] It's one of the reasons we never got on!

HENNESSY

You didn't get on? Because, you know, you've got quite a gift for getting on with people, most people, most of the time – but you didn't with Mrs T?

STEEL

Well … I didn't take to her, and she obviously didn't take to me, for very good reason. But, you know, she had to invite me to things like dinners at Number 10 and so on, and we were always perfectly civil to each other. And in fact during the Falklands War, I and David Owen accepted her private briefings, which, if you remember, Michael Foot refused. So we used to go and have a glass of whisky with her in her room. So, we got on in that sense OK – but there was no meeting of minds.

HENNESSY

Labour in the 80s has a terrible time; it turns inward, turns in on itself, and has its civil war. And Roy Jenkins comes back from Brussels[1] and makes his famous speech about the possibility of an alliance, and so on. Looking back, do you not think it would have been better, given Roy Jenkins's leanings, which were very Asquithian, if he hadn't just joined the Liberal Party, and not gone down the route of an SDP?

STEEL

We discussed that very soon after the '79 election. I went over to Brussels to see him, and I had dinner with him. His argument was that if his idea of a new party didn't come off, then he would join the Liberal Party, but it would not be in a leading role, it would just be, you know, giving us a bit of help; and I said, 'Well I don't think you should do that. I think it's more important to cause a break-out from the Labour Party, it would be much more

1 Where he was President of the European Commission

173

dramatic than simply an elder statesman joining the Liberal Party. So I didn't encourage him to join the Liberal Party, and I got a certain amount of criticism in my own party for that reason. But I still think what I did was right.

HENNESSY

And of course, you came quite close to breaking the mould, surging in the opinion polls and so on. And in the '83 election, just a per cent or so smaller share of the vote than the Labour Party. Looking back it was quite a close-run thing, the centre-left split, in terms of breaking the mould, probably perpetually.

STEEL

It was a very close-run thing, and the person who stopped it was General Galtieri. If he hadn't invaded the Falkland Islands, and Margaret Thatcher emerged as a cross between Boadicea and Britannia and therefore made her whole reputation. It wiped domestic politics off the map. I mean, we'd been winning all the by-elections, and then suddenly that stopped with the Falklands War. So, that's politics. I talked about luck earlier on –- there's bad luck as well as good luck, and that was bad luck for us.

HENNESSY

The Gang of Four – they were very interesting, Roy Jenkins, Shirley Williams, David Owen and Bill Rodgers – all very different characters. You seemed to get on naturally with Roy Jenkins. There was an affinity.

STEEL

I did get on very well with Roy. Probably I was more close to him than the other three. You know, I wasn't a rival – whereas to the other three I suppose I was.

HENNESSY

You got on pretty well with Shirley Williams and Bill Rodgers, didn't you?

STEEL

I got on perfectly well with the other three. What the more perceptive writers of that period have noted was that the great the division was between David Owen and the other three. They had all come round in various ways to the view that the SDP and the Liberal Party had to march together – in Roy's case towards union, and the other two accepted that it had to be in partnership, that there was no scope for a third and fourth party. That was never a view accepted by David Owen. So that was the division within their ranks, not with me – I had no problems with David Owen on that score; I accepted that his view and mine were different. But we got on perfectly well.

HENNESSY

You did have some problems with David Owen, because your temperaments are very different. You're essentially herbivorous, and he's a carnivore. [*Steel laughs*]

STEEL

Well, that's your way of putting it. That is how the press saw us. But the fact is that we did get on very well, you know, we stayed in each other's houses. We had problems over nuclear issues, but these were problems of policy. Although there was this divergence of view of how deeply embedded the alliance should be, we *knew* that was a difference of view that we had, and we just got on despite that.

HENNESSY

But you'll be for ever cursed in the political memory because of those wonderful puppets of *Spitting Image* of you and David Owen

– you being in his pocket and chirping away and so on. It's a cruel world, politics, for what people are remembered for; heaven forbid that it should be soon, but I can see the television the night when you go to your Liberal Paradise in the sky: that will be endlessly re-run, the *Spitting Image* of you and David Owen.

STEEL

Of course, of course. But I think we both enjoyed *Spitting Image* – he probably enjoyed it more than I did! [*Laughs*] But I used to watch it every Sunday evening, and you know, if you take these things too seriously, it's a great mistake. It was good fun. One cartoon I have on my wall in the flat is a cartoon of Trog, showing a great shark with the face of David Owen on it coming along towards this minnow, which is 'D. Steel', with the face – and suddenly, the fish swallows, and it's transformed into D Steel's face, so that in fact it's been the other way around, the minnow has swallowed the shark. And in fact, that was what happened to the SDP at the end of the day. So it's quite a clever cartoon.

HENNESSY

Is this a metaphor for you being much tougher than you appear?

STEEL

Well, that was what the cartoon implied, yes –

HENNESSY

Do you think it was right to?

STEEL

It was not a question of toughness, it was a question of having – I think – the right judgment. I think David's judgment on that whole issue was always wrong.

HENNESSY

A coalition happens, to everyone's amazement, in May 2010: the Liberals are there, in government, for the first time since the spring of 1945. It wasn't with Labour, which is where I'm sure your natural inclinations would have taken you, and always will. It's with the Conservatives. But was there not a little *frisson* of pride that your long-term aspiration for the Liberals to come in from the cold into office of a kind, albeit in a coalition, had been fulfilled?

STEEL

There was certainly a *frisson* of pride; but at the same time, I had two criticisms. One was that the whole thing was done in an unseemly rush. Five days. We took 15 days in Scotland, with a much narrower agenda, to fix a coalition. So it was done with unseemly haste; it was also done the wrong way round by talking to David Cameron first, when in fact the incumbent Prime Minister should have been talked to first. And I think if that happened, Gordon Brown would probably have come out and done his statesmanlike thing, and said he was resigning as leader of the Labour Party much earlier, and the party would have had much more clout with the Conservative Party, because they'd have been seen to be talking to their more natural allies first. So, the mechanics of it I can criticise, but you're absolutely right that the principle was correct, and the principle of holding together in a coalition in order to overcome the financial problems of the country was wholly correct.

HENNESSY

Would you rather have gone into coalition with Labour? A rainbow coalition, because you'd have needed a few others as well.

STEEL

Well I think it should have been explored a little more than it was, but you could only have done that if you'd have started the other way around.

HENNESSY

Haven't some of the coalition measures given you a bit of grief, though? People who look at the Liberal Democrat benches from across the floor of the House of Lords sometime see little bits of ... well, your faces give it away occasionally. [*Steel laughs*] I'm trying to put it tactfully. Even you, seasoned old you, gives it away sometimes!

STEEL

But the great thing about the Liberal Democrat benches at the House of Lords is that they're beyond democratic recall! [*Laughs*] They're free of responsibility. It must be very annoying for Nick Clegg, I have to say – I think he must look on them with a certain amount of justified disdain. But they do react. Their instinct is still very, very liberal. When things have gone wrong, for example the student fee debacle, which Nick Clegg has now called 'toxic' – I mean, I would have called it 'catastrophic' – then you could see the Lib Dem benches in the House of Lords, which contain a lot of experience, and a lot of dedicated people who came from the Liberal party and the SDP, tearing their hair out. But, you know, we're quite a disciplined lot, and we don't go around criticising.

HENNESSY

There was a certain *froideur* between you and Nick Clegg over the question of Lords Reform, about a largely elected House. You weren't receiving the hosannas of a grateful leader of the Liberal Democratic Party for running your alternative, organic reforms, which indeed you got.

STEEL

Our relations were a little strained; but I think one of the reasons for that was, I'd maintain, was that Nick, who's a man of great ability, doesn't really understand the constitution, and I was brought up in constitutional law. Mr Asquith never said he was going to have an elected House, he was always in favour of the supremacy of the House of Commons.

HENNESSY

Aren't you proud of your little bill, though? Because it means that peers who are convicted of serious offences bringing longer than one year of imprisonment will be gone; there's a dignified way of resigning from the chamber of the House of Lords now; and also, if you don't turn up, a persistent absentee without good reason, you're deemed to have gone, as it were. Now, it's all worth having, these organic reforms – aren't you proud of it?

STEEL

Well, yes. They're tiny measures, and they are worth having. One of the reasons I was slightly cross with Nick Clegg was that when he announced the withdrawal of his bill, I was actually sitting at home watching it on television, and some journalist, I couldn't see who it was, said, 'Well, what about the Steel bill?' And he said, 'I don't believe in legitimising the illegitimate.' And I thought that was really a bit over the top [*laughs*], and told him so! But, you know, these things are past us, and we've overcome these little difficulties.

HENNESSY

Isn't he a touch earnest for you, though?

STEEL

Well, I hope I'm earnest as well.

HENNESSY

You're pawky, as well. [*Clarifying*] P-A-W-K-Y.

STEEL

I think 'earnest' is not the right word. He's extremely able, and very quick, and sometimes just a bit too quick for his own good. [*Peter laughs*]

HENNESSY

Before we turn to an audit of your political achievements, can I raise a few of the difficulties that you've had? It's the problems on the personal side that the poor Liberal Democrats have seemed a bit prone to.

STEEL

Yes. [*Laughs*]

HENNESSY

Jeremy Thorpe – if I can put it tactfully – tragic business all that, in the mid-70s[2].

STEEL

It was a very, very sad story, Jeremy's fall from grace; and I put it down to the fact that he was very bad at choosing his friends and the people he relied on. I mean, the late Peter Bessell, who was the guy he relied on to try and deal with this unfortunate problem of this bloke … he turned to the wrong person.

HENNESSY

The other personal business that's come to haunt you is in the huge figure of Cyril Smith. The allegations are being investigated[3]. And you were Liberal leader when he surfaced in a radical newspaper

---

2 Thorpe was leader of the Liberal Party. In 1979 he was charged with conspiracy and incitement to murder, charges relating to his relationship with a former male model. He was acquitted of all charges
3 Of sexual abuse of children

in Rochdale and *Private Eye* picked it up and so on. But that's still going, isn't it? And you're still in some people's eyes in the frame because of not gripping it as Liberal party leader.

STEEL

Just let me remind you what happened. This was reported, as you say, in a radical paper in Rochdale – circulation supposedly 10,000 in the town – and repeated in *Private Eye* in 1979; they related to incidents in the 1960s, which had been investigated by the police. The local Labour Party – because he was then in the Labour Party – elected him as mayor, they got him an MBE for services to local government, he'd been elected as the MP three times – and then suddenly this appears. Apart from asking him whether this was true – and he said that yes it was, that he had been investigated by the police – there was nothing more really for me to do. Now, that was my opinion, it remains my opinion, and while people are justified in saying, 'Oh no, you should have been doing more' – quite what, I don't know – what they're not entitled to say, and this is what I object to in some of the coverage, is that somehow there was a deliberate cover-up. That I do not believe. In fact, when I did a radio interview recently on *The World At One,* I said, 'Look, I was leading a political party, not a detective agency'; a former Tory Cabinet minister who'd heard that interview said to me, 'Do you know, a friend of mine was a QC in the early 70s, and he told me he'd been given those papers by the DPP[4].' And he had sent them back with the opinion that it was not a case that he could success-fully prosecute. So I don't believe that there was a cover-up – I think there was just a decision that there was not enough concrete evidence to be able to prosecute at the time. And therefore, how was I, as leader of the party, 200 miles away from Rochdale, 20 years later – what was I supposed to do about it?

---

4 Director of Public Prosecutions

HENNESSY

Did you ever feel – if I can put it carefully – that he was a bit odd, Cyril Smith, a bit of an odd chap?

STEEL

Oh, he was.

HENNESSY

Were you at ease with him?

STEEL

He was not a soul-mate of mine. May I just remind you – because again, people forget this – when I was elected leader, he said he wouldn't speak in any constituency that had voted for me. When I was trying to form an alliance with the SDP, he said they should be strangled at birth. The idea that he was a mate of mine was ludicrous.

HENNESSY

What do you think has been your greatest political achievement?

STEEL

Oh, I'm in no doubt whatever about that. My greatest political achievement was winning Roxburgh, Selkirk and Peebles in March 1965. And I say that because if I hadn't done that none of the other things would have followed, and I would never been president of the anti-apartheid movement, I would never have gone to South Africa in charge of the Commonwealth Observer Mission at elections, I would never have done the Abortion Bill, I would never have led the party, there would never have been the Alliance. Everything stems from the fact that I had been elected to serve the people in the Borders.

HENNESSY

Being Presiding Officer of the Scottish Parliament must be up there as well.

STEEL

Very much so. When I was talking earlier about taking part in student debates, I can remember the speeches that I spoke most about were the restoration of the Scottish Parliament and the abolition of apartheid. And I lived to see both, and to play a part in both. So at the end of the day other politicians may have had power but I've had the great satisfaction of seeing my, if you like, my boyhood dreams come true, and to play a part in them. So I've had a very satisfying life.

HENNESSY

Looking back to the spring of '65 – very young Boy David, more than a little radical – and here you are now, Knight of the Thistle, Lord Steel of Aikwood. Do you think you've joined that mercurial thing called the British Establishment?

STEEL

Well, my wife keeps saying that I'm now an Establishment figure. And I suppose you can't be a Peer and a Privy Counsellor and a Knight of the Thistle and all the rest of it and not be thought of as part of the Establishment. It's rather sad, because I do remember in my campaigning days in the Borders, going round the council estates, getting all the posters on the windows and so on – I'm not sure that I could do that now, because my image is so totally changed. But I've got one political ambition left, because I was on the last train out of Galashiels, under the Beeching cuts, and I hope to be on the first train back into Galashiels next year.

HENNESSY

[*Laughing*] David Steel, thank you very much indeed.

Margaret Beckett (Dame Margaret Beckett)

Series 2, Episode 4, first broadcast 3 September 2014

Born 15 January 1943; **Educated** Notre Dame High School,
Norwich; Manchester College of Science and Technology

MP (Labour) Lincoln, 1974–79; Derby South 1983-

Assistant Government Whip, 1975–76; Parliamentary Secretary,
Department of Education and Science, 1976–79; Deputy Leader of
the Labour Party 1992–94 (acting leader May-July 1994); President
of the Board of Trade and Secretary of State for Trade and Industry,
1997–98; Lord President of the Council and Leader of the House
of Commons, 1998–2001; Secretary of State for Environment,
Food and Rural Affairs, 2001–06; Foreign and Commonwealth
Secretary, 2006–07; Minister for Housing and Planning,
Department for Communities and Local Government, 2008–09

HENNESSY

With me today is a politician who has a fistful of firsts to her credit:
first woman to be Deputy Leader of the Labour Party and for a
short spell acting leader, and the first woman to gain the glittering
prize of the Foreign Secretaryship, all over a long 40-year Westminster career where, but for a four-year gap, she sat in the House
of Commons as she does to this day, and served as a minister
under four Prime Ministers. Dame Margaret Beckett, welcome.

BECKETT

Thank you.

HENNESSY

Was yours a political home?

BECKETT

Politically aware, not politically active, perhaps partly because of my father's health, which was very poor from when I was quite small. But certainly very much politically aware, there was political chat but neither one of my parents was a party member.

HENNESSY

But there was a sort of leftish impulse …

BECKETT

Yes. My father was always 'agin the government', my mother would say.

HENNESSY

Whoever it was …

BECKETT

Indeed. [*Hennessy laughs*]

HENNESSY

Your mother was Roman Catholic, and I think you went to a Convent school?

BECKETT

I did.

HENNESSY

Did you lapse as a young woman?

BECKETT

Yes. I can identify the moment when I lapsed. I was watching Cardinal Heenan, who I think was being interviewed by John Freeman or someone like that. The final question was, 'What word would you use to sum up the Church?' And I sat there, complacently thinking, 'It will be charity or love, or something', and he said, 'Authority.' And I thought, 'That's it.'

HENNESSY

You're anti-authority in all its forms, that's very interesting.

BECKETT

It was a time of great controversy in terms of things like birth control, and a lot of anxiety about whether the church was taking the right attitudes.

HENNESSY

Looking back to your higher education, you were very much part of the coming wave. Harold Wilson made his famous 'White Heat of Technology' speech when he became the leader of the Labour Party, an extraordinary, powerful speech, and you were an engineer, a trainee engineer, a woman in a male profession, and an AEI[1] apprentice. Looking back today – it's a bit of a parody – but that's exactly what we wish the country had done in abundance, produce Margaret Becketts by the score. [*Beckett laughs*] And there you were, in the vanguard, as a young woman.

BECKETT

Yes, and I loved it. It was quite accidental. I had realised eventually, towards the end of my sixth-form career, that if one did a degree in chemistry it seem to me to be mostly organic chemistry, which bored me stiff. And the bits of chemistry I liked, actually, were in

---

1 Associated Electrical Industries

metallurgy. But in those days, there was nothing like the smooth system for applying to university that there is now, and I hadn't applied to study metallurgy. And if I'd known they were so desperate for students, I probably could have got into university in a metallurgy department. But I didn't know that, and so I started looking for employment, and I saw these apprenticeships advertised, and it sounded really interesting. So I applied, and I got one, and I ended up doing this course which was five years, pretty much – six months in college and six months on the shop floor, around the factory, which was a tremendous experience, and I absolutely loved it.

HENNESSY

I think you said once that it was a boyfriend who drew you into the Labour Party.

BECKETT

I first joined the Labour Club at college, and that was, yes, through a current boyfriend who I think was the secretary. My sister and I tried for *two years* to join the Labour Party – this was in the old days, when we were very much a voluntary organisation. Our letters and phone calls went unanswered, and then eventually we got a response.

HENNESSY

You came to national attention when you stood against Dick Taverne in the first of the two '74 elections. He'd won the famous by-election in '73, because he thought Labour's drift was leftward, and because of the anti-Europeanism he detected, and all the rest of it[2]. He was a great figure, Dick Taverne, and he had taken on, as

---

2 **Dick Taverne** was one of the few MPs elected since the Second World War who was not the candidate of a major party. In 1973, as a Labour MP, he was dissatisfied with the party's leftward direction, so he left the party and resigned his seat, forcing a by-election, which he won.

it seemed to some people, the mighty weight of the Labour movement, and prevailed. And young Margaret Jackson, as I think you still were then, was up against this shimmering figure. Did you feel somewhat intimidated?

BECKETT

No. [*Pause*]

HENNESSY

Do you not do intimidation, Margaret? [*They laugh*]

BECKETT

I'm not sure. I am the youngest of three sisters, and both my mother and my sisters, although they'd be quite put out perhaps to hear me say so, are, I think, quite formidable figures in their own right. So I used to say to my departments – 'Don't think you can bully me into something, because if sitting on me made me do things, I'd have given way years ago.'

HENNESSY

You've had always, I've felt, an instinctive loyalty to the Labour Party.

BECKETT

Yes.

HENNESSY

You're not a splitter or a quitter.

BECKETT

No.

HENNESSY

It's very much against your grain, that, isn't it?

BECKETT

Absolutely, I'm a team player. And, you know, you might say I'm scarred, I suppose: I did work at Party headquarters for some years when there were lots of rows and falling out, and blood all over the floor, and with people who had confidential documents leaking them to the media for personal advantage. Every weekend I would see people picking up the pieces from some disaster inflicted upon us by some conceited politician who had decided to do something to make themselves look good and do the Labour Party harm. I used to take pride in the fact I'd say, 'I'm a party hack.'

HENNESSY

You take it as a badge of honour to be called a party hack?

BECKETT

Absolutely, yes. [*Peter laughs*]

HENNESSY

You win in the October '74 election, you beat Dick Taverne, you come in to Westminster. Given your instincts on Europe, it must have been a bit of a strain on you in '75, with the referendum and the bulk of the Labour Cabinet saying, 'The renegotiation is fine, we've got to stay in,' and all the rest of it, and the referendum, two-thirds to one-third that we should stay in. Because you've always felt rather deeply about Europe; you certainly did in those days.

BECKETT

Oh yes, I did. I campaigned as vigorously as I could in the opposite direction. I wasn't alone, of course, there were quite a large number of people in the Party who campaigned vigorously.

HENNESSY

What was the root of your aversion to Britain in Europe?

BECKETT

I think the key thing that we felt was that these six countries[3] are not Europe, and that there would be a heavy price to be paid if Britain went into Europe, and also that the severing of our ties with the Commonwealth would be a major change. And we had other links – we had links with the EFTA[4] countries, the Scandinavians and so on. It seemed to us to be a step that we didn't need to take, and which would be a huge step in a direction in which we didn't particularly want to go, and a step that might be irrevocable.

HENNESSY

Do you think you were right? Do you think you're still the same Margaret as you were in 1975?

BECKETT

Well as it happens, the world around us has changed. If it was still the six, that would be different – but you're a bit pushed to say it's not Europe now there are 27 countries, and even at 12 or 15, particularly once the Scandinavians came in it seemed to me to be much more our sort of place.

HENNESSY

There's a Labour Party figure, Judith Hart, who's nearly forgotten now, but she was a very considerable figure, and a big shaper of you I think ...

BECKETT

Absolutely.

---

3 France, West Germany, Italy, Belgium, the Netherlands, Luxembourg
4 European Free Trade Association

HENNESSY

You were her special adviser, and then her Parliamentary Private Secretary.

BECKETT

Funnily enough, Judith was one of those politicians who was highly, highly regarded outside this country and little known within it. She had been a minister for overseas development back in the '60s, I think, or certainly a Minister at the Commonwealth Office.

HENNESSY

Commonwealth Office, yes.

BECKETT

And she became very much involved with the whole field of overseas aid and overseas development, and thought deeply about it, wrote extremely well about it, and was a passionate campaigner – as I say, respected and loved across the world.

HENNESSY

What did you learn from her?

BECKETT

I learnt that people will always assume that a woman is not the minister, and so, although it's right to be friendly and approachable, don't you forget you're the minister, or else they certainly will. I learnt that there's absolutely no reason why ministers shouldn't write their own white papers, and that indeed they might be a great deal better phrased if they did. And the third thing I learnt, which was extremely useful, was that when we first came in, in '74, she wanted to negotiate a substantial increase in the overseas aid budget, and her civil servants were totally against it. The finance people in the department were completely against it: 'You shouldn't even try, Minister, it won't do anything, and what's more, it'll do damage to our relationship with the Treasury for no useful purpose.' Anyway. Judith knew Denis Healey rather better than they did, so she did indeed successfully negotiate an increase in the budget; and I thought, in my innocence and naivety of that time, that the department would be pleased. Were they hell! They were extremely put out, because it did damage their relationship with their counterparts in the Treasury, who were very cross about it, and also, of course, because they hadn't managed to keep control of their minister. That was really a useful lesson; I've always had high regard for the Civil Service, and their professionalism, but they're not always right, especially about politicians.

HENNESSY

Your first ministerial office is Junior Minister of Education, when Joan Lestor resigned over the spending cuts in March '76, at the beginning of what was a mother and father of an economic crisis. But some of the left were very critical of you, because you were known to be of the left, and Joan was of the left, and you took her place, and there were some very unkind words spoken about you.

BECKETT

As it happens I've never had to resign. But it always seemed to me that if you resign, it should be because either there's something happening that you can't stand, and so you simply just don't want to be a part of it, or else because you hope that by resigning you force a change of some kind, and that if you do that – and Joan was campaigning about funding for nursery education – you ought to hope that whoever replaces you will want the same thing that you were trying to achieve, because otherwise, you stand less chance of achieving it. So, with the best will in the world, I never quite understood why it was such a shocking thing to do. And also, when Number 10 sent for me, I was whipping the Aircraft and Shipbuilding Bill, on which we did not have a majority because as a government we didn't have a majority. So I couldn't go. So that gave me time, which you wouldn't normally have, and I rang the chair of my local party – to whom I'm now married – and said, 'I've been asked to go to Number 10, I think it must be about this job, and I'm really not keen on the idea at all'. But we had some good friends who were absolutely *passionate* about education, people on the education committee in the county, and things like that. I took some soundings; 'What does the local party think?' The message came back loud and clear – 'Fantastic! Tell her she must take it! We can't think of anything better than for her to take that job!' So I took it.

HENNESSY

It was a very tough time, the late '70s, for the Labour Party. After Jim Callaghan had lost the election in '79, the succession for the leadership comes up – you voted for Michael Foot without hesitation.

BECKETT

Yes.

HENNESSY

Why was that?

BECKETT

I liked Denis Healey very much, and if it had been a few years earlier I might have voted for Denis. You know, he was a brilliant man and all that. But – [*pause*] Denis didn't seem to be able to draw people round him, and I thought that, whatever his fine qualities, the Labour Party needed people to draw people together.

HENNESSY

Perhaps it's slightly more surprising, looking at it from the outside, that you voted for Tony Benn in the Deputy Leadership election, and didn't vote for Denis Healey then either.

BECKETT

Well, no, because I worked with Tony. When I was working for the Labour Party on economic and industrial policy Tony was the Shadow Cabinet minister that we worked with, and we all worked very closely on a whole string of economic stuff, and so I knew him well and closely. And I was out of Parliament at that time. I just thought Tony had got lots of ideas, a fresh approach to the party, and that he could be a good Deputy Leader.

HENNESSY

But given your instincts towards unity and loyalty, which are very powerful, as you've described them, the Healey-Foot combination would have been a much more balanced, unifying thing than Benn-Foot. The Benn-Foot combination, to some people's thinking, would have meant that the '83 loss in the general election would have been even greater.

BECKETT

I can see that; but there is another factor that was very much so then, and has become less so now, which was: if you were on the right, you voted for the candidate on the right whoever that was, and if you were on the left, you voted for the candidate of the left, whoever that was. Things are a little more thoughtful now I think.

HENNESSY

[Laughing] That's a very delicate way of putting it. In the '80s, the Miners' Strike had a tremendous, searing effect within the Labour movement. But if I remember, you were a member of the campaign group which supported Arthur Scargill. Did you have reservations about all of that?

BECKETT

It was an incredibly difficult period, and that probably was a low point, a very difficult time. I think it was hard for all of us, because none of us wanted the damage that was being done to continue, the damage to the mining community apart from anything else. And yet there was a very clear sort of feeling of, 'Were you on the miners' side or where you against them?' Whatever you thought about the judgments Arthur was making there was no question: I was on the miners' side.

HENNESSY

Can I ask you about nuclear weapons? You've always been by instinct a disarmer, as I think most people are, it's just the *kind* of disarmament that the argument's about, I think, multilateral or unilateral. You were a member of the Campaign for Nuclear Disarmament as a unilateralist; but Neil Kinnock managed to move the Labour Party away from that position. Did you move with him? Or did you stay a member of CND?

BECKETT

I can't quite remember. I think I stayed a member of the CND at that time. But bear in mind, I joined CND when there was no other game in town it seemed to me. And the notion that there would ever be any multilateral disarmament seemed so far beyond any realistic expectation that there was almost a feeling that people who said, 'Well, I'm in favour of multilateral disarmament, not unilateralism,' weren't serious. You know, it was an excuse not to say, 'Actually, I don't care about nuclear disarmament'. And if you were serious, the only way to show it was to be willing for Britain to stand alone if need be.

HENNESSY

Stand alone without nuclear weapons, yes?

BECKETT

Yes. Of course, things changed dramatically: we did see multilateral moves. The second thing that changed, I'm afraid, and this is the point at which I left the CND, was that it became clear that CND had become a pacifist organisation, because whatever I felt about nuclear weapons I've never been a pacifist.

HENNESSY

And I remember in December 2006, when you were Foreign Secretary in Tony Blair's Cabinet, the Cabinet takes the decision that there shall be a successor set of boats to Trident, to carry on into the 2050s if need be. Because you were one of the lead ministers, you and Des Browne, the Defence Secretary. Was there not a CND pang, Margaret?

BECKETT

Yes, there was a pang.

HENNESSY

Did you express it in the Cabinet Room?

BECKETT

No, no, it was a joint White Paper. We in our departments had worked on it together. So one went through the thinking and the concerns, and it seemed to me that this was not the time. However, it was quite interesting because in that White Paper we also committed ourselves to saying there should be a much stronger move towards multilateral nuclear disarmament on the part of all those who were the nuclear-weapon states. And I think people thought we'd put that in as a sop to the Labour Party, but we didn't, we meant it. And the very last thing which I did as Foreign Secretary, of which I am extremely proud, was to be able to make a speech on behalf of a serving British government, committing ourselves to a world free of nuclear weapons. Perhaps not next week, but committing ourselves to work *in government* for a world free of nuclear weapons – which actually did, I'm told, lead to a whole lot of the initiatives like Global Zero that are going on now.

HENNESSY

Spooling back to the '90s, you become Deputy Leader of the Labour Party, which suggests, Margaret, that you had within you some kind of desire to be Prime Minister if you could be one day. When did you acquire the feeling that you might want to do it, you might be quite good at it?

BECKETT

I didn't acquire the feeling that I might be able to do it and might be quite good at it until after I'd been leader ...

HENNESSY

Acting leader after John Smith's death ...

BECKETT

Yes. I had no intention of being the Deputy Leader, and no desire, either. But after the '92 defeat, when John began to run for the leadership – it was a Sunday afternoon, and we'd heard on the radio or something, or television, that John Smith and I were running as a team for the Leader and Deputy Leader. We weren't. And so I rang the BBC and said, 'I don't know where you've got that from.' And a little while later my telephone rang, and it was a Parliamentary colleague, and he said, 'I've rung you about the Deputy Leadership.' And I said, 'It's all nonsense, I'm not running.' 'Yes,' he said, 'I've heard that – what I want to know is, why not?' And after that, the phone just kept ringing with people saying, 'You've got to stand.' And eventually, I gave way. And John came into my office and said, 'I came in this morning determined to tell you that you've got to run; but I gather you've already decided to.'

HENNESSY

I remember, when you opened your campaign, after John Smith's early death, for the leadership, you said something that struck me very much at the time, not least because I thought it was probably autobiographical. You said, 'We need to alter the political climate and set people free to have their heads in the clouds even while their feet stay firmly on the floor.' That's you, isn't it?

BECKETT

[*Laughing*] I suppose it is! Not that I thought of it at the time.

HENNESSY

But it's your general approach to politics, isn't it?

BECKETT

Yes, I think it probably is. It may be because I didn't study politics. I'm just somebody who joined the Labour Party.

HENNESSY

That's probably an advantage, not to study politics. [*Margaret laughs*]

BECKETT

But it's one of the reasons, I think, why the feet are firmly on the ground. Because I came into politics almost by accident: I just joined the Labour Party and then people kept asking me to do things. And so I've always been there for what you can achieve; get the maximum out of it that you possibly can, but it's getting something. Someone said to me a while ago, about a different colleague: 'He's one of those people who thinks if he feels that he's won the intellectual argument, he doesn't mind whether he wins the decision.' And I looked aghast, and this person who'd worked with both of us chuckled, and I said, 'Yes, and I'm the other way around'. [*Laughs*] Of course I want to win the argument; but it's the decision I want.

HENNESSY

You enjoyed being a minister, didn't you?

BECKETT

Yes.

HENNESSY

You were President of the Board of Trade, you were at Defra[5] … you had a whole range of things before you went to the Foreign Office. You are a lady of government really, aren't you Margaret?

BECKETT

Yes. I've always enjoyed making decisions. I like the challenge.

HENNESSY

You became very concerned about climate change, global warming.

BECKETT

Absolutely.

HENNESSY

Do you think that's where you made the most difference?

BECKETT

I think it probably is, because I worked out once that – with agriculture and environment – I'd done something like 14 sets of international negotiations. So yes, I think that's where we made a substantial difference.

HENNESSY

What do you think it takes to be a negotiator? Because you must have spent hours in negotiations of various kinds.

BECKETT

You need to completely understand your own position, and what

---

5 Department of Environment, Food and Rural Affairs

it is that you've got to have and what you can't live with. You need to understand as much as you can the same context about other people's position, and then you need to listen. Because often what somebody *isn't* saying gives you the clue that, 'Ah, they're not quite so worried about that'. That's the opportunity, that's the opening.

HENNESSY

This negotiating experience is probably one of the reasons why Tony Blair made you Foreign Secretary – but you were immensely surprised. It's reported at the time that your reaction was terse, and rather in the expletive department.

BECKETT

I am afraid so, yes. I understand Jack Straw said much the same when he was appointed.

HENNESSY

You were really thrown by this, you didn't expect it?

BECKETT

I hadn't given any thought to where, if he did move me, he might move me to. So I was a bit stunned.

HENNESSY

It was a terribly difficult inheritance, the Foreign Secretary-ship always is; it's as if there's ten simultaneous chess games going. [*Beckett laughs*] And at least five of the boards are on fire, I always thought. And you have to start running, you can't just say, oh I'll think about it for a month or two.

BECKETT

I was appointed on Friday, and on Monday I was in the States meeting Condi Rice, Sergey Lavrov, the German and French

Foreign Ministers, and the Chinese Foreign Minister, all to talk about Iran.

HENNESSY

People think that Tony Blair pretty well wanted to be his own Foreign Secretary. It can't have been the easiest of jobs, being a Foreign Secretary under a Prime Minister that not only had his own advisers in Number 10, but also was quite a big player in the world and thought he should be.

BECKETT

I rather liked him being a big player in the world. He and I had worked together a lot on climate change because he was one of the few world leaders who'd got it, and was prepared to campaign and do the work, and do the networking and so on that was necessary. And so I admired that. I didn't feel in any way constrained or bothered.

HENNESSY

There was an occasion when Israel invaded Lebanon, and the Labour Party was very critical of the Labour government not coming out and saying anything about it. Was that a bit of a strain for you?

BECKETT

It was one of these occasions, which happens perhaps more these days in politics, where the media decide that you have to use a particular set of words, and they decide to show their authority. We had to call for an unconditional ceasefire, and everybody knew that meant Israel had to stop fighting but that Hezbollah didn't. And we all said, all the Foreign Ministers, 'Cessation of violence' … 'End to conflict' … all manner of words that meant both sides should stop. But that wasn't good enough. If we didn't say 'Unconditional ceasefire' we wanted the bloodshed to continue. It was absolutely ridiculous. And in fact some of my staff told me that the final meeting of the Security Council, that did bring an end to the conflict, principally happened because I insisted. We were being advised that nothing's moving in New York, 'Nothing's happening – you'll be embarrassed if you come here'. And I said, 'I'm not going through another weekend. Terrible things can happen, I am going to New York.' And I rang Condoleezza Rice, and she said, 'Well my lot tell me not to go'. I said, 'So do mine, but I'm going.' And she said, 'Well, if you're going, I'll come.' And we rang round the others and we got that final decision made. And my staff tell me they thought it would not have happened then if I hadn't taken that stand. So we all cared terribly about it. But how do you get the maximum influence, to get people to listen, to stop the bloodshed? It mattered more to me that we had real influence in trying to bring the bloodshed to an end than that we got press praise for saying something in a way that might have done more harm than good. That's what always really matters to me.

HENNESSY

When the Blair years are looked at, however far ahead, it will be Iraq that will be up there in technicolor, as you well know. We haven't had the Chilcot report, the benefit of it, as we are talking now; but looking back, Margaret, are you confident that the full Cabinet tested out intelligence on weapons of mass destruction and the legal opinion of the Attorney General?

BECKETT

I felt that we had been kept very fully informed of the progress of the negotiations, at the United Nations and wherever else they were. Both Jack and Tony kept the Cabinet very well informed.

HENNESSY

Jack Straw …

BECKETT

Yes. And so we were familiar with the issues. We didn't see the early discussions, but I mean, I have seen now some of Peter Goldsmith's opinion and you get this with lawyers – 'On one hand, on the other hand'…

HENNESSY

Goldsmith being the Attorney General …

BECKETT

But what matters is their *final* opinion. And it seemed clear to me he was an honourable man, and this was absolutely his final opinion. On the intelligence, we all had the briefings. And one thing that stuck in my mind – and he's said it publicly now, so I feel able to say it – is that Peter Hain was at that Cabinet, and he said that he was convinced by the intelligence on the weapons of mass destruction because of the time he'd spent in the Foreign Office, which was when Robin Cook was Foreign Secretary. Robin was the one who said he wasn't convinced by it, but he never said it in Cabinet.

HENNESSY

Didn't he?

BECKETT

I mean I wasn't astonished when Robin resigned, because he had *hated* being moved from the Foreign Office. But I thought, 'I obviously wasn't listening carefully enough when he'd said how important a second resolution was'.

HENNESSY

That's a specific UN resolution authorising the use of force …

BECKETT

A specific one. Lots of people said how important a second resolution was *if you could get it.* Nobody dissented from that. But I
never remembered Robin saying something that made me think,
'He's implying that if we don't get a second resolution, he'll go'.
And when Andrew Turnbull, the Cabinet Secretary at the time,
gave evidence to the Chilcot Inquiry, he said that Robin Cook
had never said anything to Cabinet that gave that impression. But
there's something else that comes out of some of the evidence to
Chilcot. I had not known, until I read some of that evidence before
I gave evidence myself, that the Foreign Office legal team *at the
United Nations*, the people who were the *UN* legal experts, who'd
dealt with all the negotiation on the resolutions, believed that the
first resolution gave you authority to go to war. They did not agree
with the people back in London, some of whom resigned over it,
who said that it was illegal without a second resolution. The people
who actually negotiated the first resolution and were up to their
ears in the detail of that, and the way things work at the UN, didn't
agree.

HENNESSY

If Robin Cook had spoken up in the way that he might have done
in the full Cabinet, would that have given you pause?

BECKETT

[*Pause*] Probably not, because, with great respect to Robin, who
was a brilliant man, he was disappointed and unhappy. I mean, it
would have given me pause – but we believed that we were taking
the decision on the evidence that was before us, and evidence that
everybody else in the world believed.

HENNESSY

You set quite a style as Foreign Secretary – people rather liked
your caravanning holidays. [*Beckett laughs*]

HENNESSY

Did your Special Branch mind?

BECKETT

They loved it.

HENNESSY

Did they have to sit in a little caravan beside your big one?

BECKETT

It wasn't quite as straightforward as that, but basically they were around. They claim they thoroughly enjoyed it.

HENNESSY

Margaret, what trace would you like to leave on history, and what trace do you think you will leave on political history?

BECKETT

[*Laughs*] Probably none. I'm very cynical about how much impact politicians make, in the great sweep of history. What trace would I like to leave ... I mean there are some things I'm very proud to have been involved with: the minimum wage is one; the progress we made on climate change; the stuff on nuclear weapons. I think I'd like to be remembered as somebody who tried to make the world a better place for people who need someone to speak up for them.

HENNESSY

If I could give you one last great reform, wave a magic wand for you, what would it be?

BECKETT

It would be nuclear disarmament.

HENNESSY

Margaret, thank you very much.

David Owen (Lord Owen)

Series 3, Episode 1, first broadcast 13 July 2015

Born 2 July 1938; **Educated** Bradfield College; Sidney Sussex College, Cambridge; St Thomas' Hospital, London

MP (Labour) Plymouth Sutton 1966–74; Plymouth Devonport 1974–92 (SDP 1981–92).

Parliamentary Secretary for Defence (Royal Navy), Ministry of Defence, 1968–70; Parliamentary Secretary, Department of Health and Social Security, 1974; Minister of State DHSS, 1974–76; Minister of State, Foreign and Commonwealth Office 1976–77; Foreign and Commonwealth Secretary, 1977–79. Co-founder, SDP, 1981; Leader of the SDP, 1983–87, 1988–92.

Autobiography *Time to Declare*, 1991

HENNESSY

With me today is David Owen, Lord Owen, one of the most vivid and flavourful politicians of the post-war years, who, after becoming Foreign Secretary at the age of 38 in the Callaghan government of the 1970s, spent a good part of the 1980s attempting to reshape the centre-left in Britain, as one of the co-founders of the Social Democratic Party. He now sits in the House of Lords as an independent social democrat. David, welcome.

OWEN

It's nice to be here.

HENNESSY

Tell me about your family formation. You were born near Plymouth to a Welsh mother and with family in Wales, which I think probably had a very considerable influence on you. Were you in effect brought up in the Welsh radical tradition, even though you lived in the South West?

OWEN

Well, in the Welsh radical tradition in the sense that politics is important and is discussed a huge amount. My father was a general practitioner and he was an independent on the parish council; my mother was an independent on Devon County Council and an alderman, and a real independent. In those days, she wasn't a closet Tory, she had her own views, and was very powerfully involved with the mentally handicapped and with health issues for the county council. So politics was discussed, but very rarely in a party-political sense. But my father summed it up pretty well by saying, 'Nobody in our family has ever voted Conservative without a stiff drink before and afterwards.' I think that was basically our attitude.

HENNESSY

But you spent holidays with the Welsh family?

OWEN

Yes, in the early days we used to always try and spend Christmas together, and in the summer we'd often go to Tenby, or particularly to Aberporth. And I lived with my grandmother and my grandfather, who was a clergyman, blind, in the Welsh church but basically a Methodist, needed the Welsh church, therefore was very keen on disestablishment. And I went to the local school every day with him, as he tapped his way on the road down to the village church. And I learnt Welsh, but I've forgotten every word of it! So I do identify with the Welsh; I feel Welsh, I have no English blood in me at all.

HENNESSY

There is, I think, an ancestor of yours, your great-grandfather, who had early things to say about remaking the centre-left in Britain.

OWEN

Well, he was chairman of Glamorgan County Council, as a prominent Liberal. I mean he really did know Lloyd George.

HENNESSY

Early part of the 20th century?

OWEN

Yes, he died in 1923. He was the Chairman of Ogmore Vale Liberal Party; but also, interestingly, he was Chairman of Ogmore Vale Divisional Liberal and *Labour* party, and before that mid-Glamorgan. Those were the days when a strong Liberal Party, the government, was still ready to do seat deals with the small Labour Party, if it would increase their representation.

HENNESSY

The NHS has, I think, been your life-long cause, and I think you picked it up around the table at home, didn't you? Were your mother and father shot through with the altruism of the NHS in its original conception?

OWEN

Yes, my father came back from the war, voted Labour because he wanted a national health service; he genuinely wanted to give up having to charge patients whom he knew couldn't afford for him to come and have a consultation with them in their home.

And all his life he supported it, though he was critical of it from time to time. So it is, if you like, in my DNA, and I couldn't have imagined what's happened to the health service since about 2002: it started under Tony Blair, and it continued under Cameron, and who knows, but I personally think we have destroyed the National Health Service.

HENNESSY

Through market-isation, a terrible word.

OWEN

Yes, but it's accurate. 'Privatisation' isn't quite correct. There was very little privatisation. They've kept the assets, they've kept the name, 'the National Health Service'. But what they've brought in is the American market structures, and it's a recipe, actually, for spending far more of a percentage of GDP on health, but inefficiently and unfairly. Any health service is going to be rationed; the key thing is, do you ration it through the market or do you ration it through a combination of democracy, good health priorities and a little flexibility. I am quite keen on the idea of looking now at devolving big chunks of the Health Service to some of the big city conurbations in England, and I'd do it to the Mayor of London as well. So in that sense, I suppose, I'm a radical; I've been arguing this for quite some years.

HENNESSY

Was your radicalism enhanced, as a young man, by the Suez Crisis? It affected your generation pretty strongly.

OWEN

It hugely affected me. I remember it very well. My parents believed that you should work your way through university, and so I was working at Costain, the builders, on the sewage plant in Plymouth – which, when we go past it, my children all think I built

single-handedly [*laughs*], they pull my leg. However, it still exists.
But the Suez Crisis broke …

You were 18 …

I was 18. Nasser nationalised the Suez Canal and he was ready
to pay compensation to all shareholders at the same price as the
day before nationalisation; it seemed to me, therefore, that it was
something not to get this worked up about, and the idea of going
to war over it seemed ridiculous. So I went with my workers, fellow
workers, having sandwiches for lunch, and I was staggered to find
that they were totally on the side of the Tory government and Sir
Anthony Eden, and against the 'gyppos' as they called them, and
all in favour of sending troops in to the Suez Canal. And I first discovered what you could call 'working-class Toryism' – in which the
dockyard cities, Plymouth of course being famously one of them,
are very strong. And therefore you have to get to grips with the fact
that you couldn't assume liberal views, liberal with a small 'l', were
always going to be held by members of the Labour Party, far from it.
I remember first canvassing in my constituency in Plymouth in the
'66 election, and the door being slammed in my face, saying, 'We're
for Queen and Country here'. That meant they were Tories. I soon
learned to put my foot in the door and say, 'Well, I'm for Queen and
Country too!' [*laughs*] and then to try and get an argument going.

What made you want to be a medical student? Was it the family
tradition again?

I changed late, really. I was nearly 17 before I decided to do
medicine. I was going to do law but I took a rather prissy view;

I discovered that you have to defend people even if you thought they were guilty – probably a rather simplistic view. I think initially I didn't want to just do medicine – there were a huge number of doctors and clergymen in our family, typically Welsh, and I thought law was going to be more interesting. My grandfather was also very keen on the law at one time. But I switched and I've never regretted it. My wife jokes that when an election was called – and Plymouth was a pretty marginal seat for a while – I would look up the vacancies for neurologists in the back of a *British Medical Journal*, just in case. I never could take it for granted that I was going to win my seat. The majority was down to 400–700 ... pretty tight at times.

HENNESSY

It must have been an advantage, though, knowing that you had a proper profession to fall back on if the caprice of the electoral system or your electorate threw you out.

OWEN

Yes, you could earn more money, and you would go back to something you loved. Yes it was a tremendous – and I suspect it's been one of the reasons why I have felt freer. I've not felt that the party Whip was an absolute in my political life.

HENNESSY

You made rapid progress, having come in in the '66 election; Minister of the Navy about two years later, Harold Wilson appointing you. And you worked with the extraordinary Denis Healey in the Ministry of Defence.

OWEN

Well, 'extraordinary', I don't know if that's the right word for him. I think he's a fantastic character, I love him to bits, really. He was a wonderful boss, I learned a huge amount from him.

HENNESSY

What did you learn from him?

OWEN

I think an integrity of ideas. The trouble with Denis is that there are two Denises: in opposition, you can do anything you like, it doesn't matter; in government, you've got to be very serious. [*Laughing*] But I don't think you can be quite so dismissive of what you do in opposition. But he is both an intellectual and a man of the people. Long may we have people like him in politics. And I respect and admire him. Of course we've slagged each other off in public, we've had some quite serious rows. But underneath it, my wife and his wife, and Denis and I, have always got on.

HENNESSY

He could be fairly rude about you: he once called you Mrs Thatcher in trousers, which for him was not a compliment.

OWEN

No. And I didn't accept it as a compliment. But it was at a time when I was fighting the Labour Party, and Denis had decided to stay. I respected those people who had broadly the same views ...

HENNESSY

This is the mid-80s now ...

OWEN

I mean, if Denis had fought Michael Foot in '80 for the leadership of the party, which he'd have lost, but if he'd fought him on the issues instead of trying to stand as a compromising candidate, I think he would have very soon – certainly before the election – replaced Michael Foot and become the leader of the Labour Party, and we would have been standing with somebody who had been fighting for the things we wanted, and I certainly don't think I would have left to join the SDP. The appalling problem that we were faced with was the 1983 manifesto. People find it very difficult to remember. I could never have fought the election, on the '83 manifesto in Plymouth – they'd have voted me out. And they should have voted me out! I'd been asked to support giving up on nuclear deterrence, which went right to the heart of the nuclear-submarine build rate; to come out of the European Community, as it was then called, without even a referendum, which Labour itself had only given seven years earlier in '75; and I'd been hugely involved in these issues as Foreign Secretary. To suddenly turn 180 degrees on two major, massive, issues of importance to Britain, to fight on that manifesto in '83, I couldn't have done. So, for me, the issue was 'Do I stay in politics? Or do I stand and fight with a new party?' And that was the issue.

HENNESSY

You made great cause early on in your Parliamentary life with another very great figure of the centre-left, Roy Jenkins. And I think you resigned with Roy over the idea of a referendum on Britain's membership of the European Union when you were in opposition in the early 70s. You were very close to Roy Jenkins.

OWEN

Yes, I was very close to him, and we did resign. Actually, we disagreed: I argued on paper, in detail, for accepting that referendum, Roy argued against, very powerfully. And at one stage I could see he wasn't taking my argument seriously, because I think he thought I was trying to hedge my bets and not have to resign. And I said to him, 'Look Roy, I am resigning anyhow. If you resign, I'm going too. That's out of loyalty. Let's argue this issue out on its merits.' In these sort of areas he was very good, and he saw the issue straight, and I resigned with him. I resigned a number of times, actually, probably a little too often. [*Hennessy laughs*] But I always think you resign for a purpose, and that was certainly a resignation for a purpose; in fact, they've all been for a purpose, my resignations.

HENNESSY

It's interesting because your critics, David, say that it's a great characteristic that you do feel things very strongly, hence all those resignations, but that in argument, in which you're very powerful, you don't just want to win but you want to flatten the opposition. Do you think that's true of you? They've always said that about you, because you have a force field around you.

OWEN

You frequent these circles of people who say this about me. [*Laughs*] I don't think that's true. I mean, sometimes, in government I quite often took on an issue which I didn't totally agree with myself, but in order to provoke an argument. I enjoy argument, personally; I also find it clears my mind. I like the confrontational side of politics. I like the House of Commons as it used to be. Nothing is more thrilling really than winding up a debate, in the old days, at 9.30pm, speaking for 29 minutes and having to sit down, to shouting and cat-calling and a great many people who are not just at the bar, but they've been at other bars before they're at the bar – and the thing is a cockpit, and that's a part of politics I still think needs to be retained in part. I'm not wanting the flattening out of all differences. I don't – I'm a militant moderate.

HENNESSY

[*Laughs*] Who loves a scrap.

OWEN

I don't mind a fight.

HENNESSY

You again rose rapidly in the Wilson and Callaghan governments as Minister of Health, and then when Tony Crosland dies in '77 you become Foreign Secretary, at a very young age, 38, I think the youngest since Anthony Eden. Do you think, looking back, that it came to you too soon?

OWEN

Well, in part it did, obviously, because you haven't got the same maturity and length of history. On the other hand, you've got courage, vigour, and capacity for hard work. It's a stretching job, and in those days there were a lot of very nasty world confrontations that needed a great deal of travel, yet you also have young children and a family. Personally it was a great decision to be given that responsibility – but I think on balance it was a good thing to have it young.

HENNESSY

Do you think you were a bit rough on the officials?

OWEN

No, I don't think so at all.

HENNESSY

Some of them thought you were.

OWEN

They did, yes, but then some of them find a difficulty in accepting the policy of the government – not my policy, the policy of the government – and particularly so on Europe. Actually, I had no problem with the diplomats on Africa, and they were solid to a man. I was the first Foreign Secretary to be utterly clear: one person, one vote, no A-rolls, B-rolls ...

HENNESSY

In Rhodesia ...

OWEN

In Rhodesia, and also in Namibia, which was another big issue, and South Africa itself ... you know, the whole of southern Africa was in flame, it was a very tricky issue. But we were also dealing with real issues with the Soviet Union and the Cold War. But on Europe, these people who'd spent many years negotiating and having to renegotiate – a rather strange and not a very significant negotiation happened in 1975 – found it difficult that the Labour Party was still not a federalist party. That was a Cabinet decision, and I'm very pleased to have been asked to present the papers for that Cabinet decision in the summer of 1977. I think it's the only time where there has been a very coherent strategy of how we saw our membership of the European Union. I was in favour of Europe, and remain in favour of Europe; but there is no way that I'm going to be integrated to such an extent that you end up in a federalist Europe, and you've lost the sinews of nationhood, if you like, of being an independent state.

HENNESSY

If Jim Callaghan had won the '79 election, I think he would have asked you to be Chancellor of the Exchequer. He was going to split the Treasury into a Ministry of Finance and then a Bureau of the Budget, and put Roy Hattersley into one and you in the other. Did he tell you that you were going to be Chancellor if he won?

OWEN

No, but I think there are some signs that that was what he was going to do. But who knows? These are the 'ifs' of history.

HENNESSY

Yes, we have to be careful with the 'ifs' of history – but if Jim had won, and you had become Chancellor of the Exchequer, you'd have been on a pretty good glide path, albeit with others wanting to be on the glide path too, to replace him, and become Prime Minister one day.

OWEN

Look, I gave up the possibility of being Prime Minister the day I agreed to join the SDP.

HENNESSY

Yes, but that came a bit later.

OWEN

That came later, yes, two years later. I think it's easier, actually, to give up these possibilities, and they are only possibilities, if you've had one of the great offices of state, and I remember when ambition changed a little for me. One night, Field Marshal Carver, who was then the designate Governor for Rhodesia, and Sir Antony Duff who later came to head up MI5 – these two very senior and very admired-by-me men came to see me, and they said, 'You always said you wouldn't call a conference at Lancaster House until you were sure it would succeed,'[1] and at that stage, in October, November of 1978 everybody was wanting it. Callaghan wanted it, Jimmy Carter wanted it. But there was only one answer to that question: it won't succeed. So I said, 'Well, I'll think about it.' And I decided that it couldn't go ahead, and I had to persuade Jim against having that conference. And from that moment on, I passed a certain threshold. It was strongly in my interests to be the chairman of that conference, but it was premature, and these people were right. And I think that, when you've taken office like

---

1 The conference was tasked with settling the Rhodesia crisis and bringing internationally recognised independence, following Ian Smith's unilateral declaration of independence in 1965. It would finally take place – under a Conservative government – in 1980

that there are moments when you do stop being a purely partisan, party politician – you have to look at the wider interests. Not being pompous about it at all, you do grow a little in stature and in worth, and I think that was a moment. And from then on I always felt, 'Look – I've had this fantastic experience, I've had this fantastic opportunity, it's not the end of the world if you don't become Prime Minister'. Of course I'd like to have been! But it didn't eat me up.

HENNESSY

Labour in '79 is in bad shape after the elections, going into a civil war, and you leave, for reasons we've already talked about. Was it a wrench, leaving the Labour Party, David? Didn't you really rather love the Labour Party?

OWEN

Huge, huge wrench. About the middle 1990s, '95, '96, Jim Callaghan used to say to me, when we'd meet, 'David, I think it's time you came back to the Labour Party, come back to us.' He never criticised me for joining the SDP. And I suddenly had a leaflet in an envelope, not a single sign of who it came from, and it was the leaflet of the young Dr David Owen, fighting Torrington in the 1964 General Election, pristine new leaflet, just folded.

HENNESSY

You never knew who sent it?

OWEN

I never knew who sent it. It had a North Devon postmark on it. It came from someone in the Labour Party. I have a few ideas of who it could have been. And … and I wept, actually, when I looked at that. Even to talk about it is quite difficult, quite emotional. These were wonderful people in the Labour Party. Largely non-conformist, very Welsh in a way, holding their faith. The only issue for me then was whether I could save my deposit. There wasn't the slightest chance of winning in '64 in that particular seat. And it was very medieval England, you went into a square with a loudspeaker, it was a one-man-and-a-boy organisation really. You'd start speaking about the Labour Party and the Labour slogans, and you'd see the curtains just move. They wouldn't come out to see you, but they would come and listen. If you held your faith in those sort of constituencies, all through those years, it was a deep faith, and it was a good faith. It was about trying to achieve a fairer world, a fairer country, a fairer town, city; these were people who were often practising their religious views through their political party. They were really good people. And they still exist, let's be clear about that – they still exist in the Labour Party, and the Labour Party has to ignite their commitment and their passion again.

HENNESSY

I can see it's affecting you; as we Catholics say, there's a twitch on the thread. Would you go back? Can you go back?

OWEN

To the Labour Party?

HENNESSY

Yes ...

OWEN

I consider that I'm more or less back with the Labour Party. To join the Labour Party officially would mean, because I'm in the House of Lords, taking the Whip. I don't really like the House of Lords, I think it's there for a purpose, which in my view is a few debates on foreign policy a year and some other ethical and moral issues. I don't really want to go back to voting on a Whip, and that's what it would mean. But I have given the Labour Party money in the last couple of years. I was deeply upset that they couldn't campaign with the passion and unity which I wanted it to on the National Health Service. I was very sad. I think it would have given them the edge, but they were still hung up with one section of the party wanting markets in healthcare, and another section not wanting to, and I hope they resolve that issue in at least the next few months. No, I want to see them back. I'm in mourning, really. I still wish that Ed Miliband would have been in Number 10, and it wouldn't have worried me at all if you'd have had to work with the SNP, and Greens and the Liberal Party and Uncle Tom Cobley and all.

HENNESSY

Looking back to the SDP experience, the Alliance came very close to getting the second-largest share of the vote in the '83 election. It was a close run thing – the mould nearly did fracture. And yet you fell out amongst yourselves, particularly you and Roy Jenkins, which will mystify people looking back because the difference between you on policy – style is a different question – was minute. And here was this great figure, who'd been a bit of a beacon for you – it must be very tough, David, looking back at that.

OWEN

[*Pause*] Yes, it's tough. The issue was a very simple one. We who were young and had a lot to lose were giving up the Labour Party, giving up the chances of being in senior office, because we thought we could recreate an opposition as a Social Democratic Party that would be identified with Socialist International. That was the party that Roy Jenkins joined with me. And within weeks we discovered it was actually that they wanted to have a party which could have joint membership with the Liberals. If that had been on offer, a lot of us wouldn't have dreamt of joining it. Now, I'm not regretting the SDP, the SDP was in many ways a marvellous vehicle for bringing people into politics who'd never been in it before, particularly women; and giving women a strong stance in party policy.

But Roy was a Liberal, and wanted a joint party with the Liberals. That's absolutely fine, but don't fly under those colours. That was not what we signed up for, the Gang of Four. The Gang of Four was for a social democratic party.

HENNESSY

It was painful reading, reading his memoirs, and yours. There was the question of nuclear weapons and so on – he was rather direct about you, claiming you were building a philosophy around a weapons system. He was very cutting to you, and you were really quite cutting back. Do you think there was any way you could have avoided that falling-out?

OWEN

I think sometimes in politics these deeper divisions that exist in the group are highlighted by the personalities of the leaders – in a way you see that with Lloyd George and Asquith – and maybe … maybe it could have been different, I don't know. Of course I believed it would have been different: I didn't want to be the leader of the SDP, I wanted Shirley Williams to be the leader, I begged her to stand, I begged her to stand, she and Roy. However, she wouldn't stand, and it was for me a huge tragedy. If she'd stood then, she'd have been the leader of the party, we'd have been a clearly social democratic party, we'd have had much more appeal to the Labour Party in the North East, to women in the Labour Party, we'd have done even better in the election of '83, and I think she would have stayed. I would have supported her right the way through to the next election in '87. But, you know, these are the 'ifs' of history, and there were a lot of personal reasons, which I am now much more aware of, why Shirley didn't want to take the leadership, and I respect those; but it was a tragedy. Then she quite understandably moved more towards the Liberals and towards Roy Jenkins's few, because she was out of Parliament, she was looking for a seat. And it was perfectly understandable. But what do I do? I'm in a seat which I have taken away from the Labour Party. I could win Plymouth, Devonport as a Social Democrat; I couldn't win it as a Liberal. The Liberals are strong in Devon, Cornwall and Somerset, but they're nothing in Plymouth. Callaghan used to say that in politics everything depends on where you sit, by which he meant which constituency you're in. If you're very ambitious in the West Country, in my day when the Liberals were getting the seats, and you are on the progressive side, become a Liberal. But I didn't become a Liberal, for a lot of reasons: I respect the collective decision-making, the collective nature, of the Labour Party. I'm not at all ashamed of the links between the Labour Party and the trade unions. I find myself now being looked on as wildly left [*laughing*] by quite a lot of my friends. I don't think I've really shifted my position. But you're right; Roy and I did break our relationship, from being very close. It was not easy, probably, for him to become President of the Commission and find that this young political figure, to whom he was really a mentor, was suddenly the Foreign Secretary, chairing the Council of Foreign Ministers. So that tension started from '77 ... it was there a few years before that.

HENNESSY

That's when Roy Jenkins went to the European Commission ...

OWEN

He went there, and I thought rightly, and I think he was a good President of the Commission. I think it would have been better, in retrospect, if he had joined the Liberal Party a little earlier, while still in Brussels, and come to an agreement with David Steel; and if we had broken off, we would have been much clearer that we were people doing a deal on seats, a pact. This merger – I don't understand where it comes from. We were told you couldn't have more than three parties; now you've got five or six.

HENNESSY

Ralf Dahrendorf, a great observer of British politics and, I suspect a friend of yours, once said that the SDP promised people a better yesterday.

OWEN

It was a wounding phrase, and it was, unfortunately, too true. And there again, the problem really was Roy. Not totally him, by any means, but he came of an age where he was very committed to certain things, and the party wanted to move towards more of a market in the private sector. He wanted a prices-and-incomes policy. That was ridiculous; we'd been through prices-and-incomes policies. They had patently failed by then. The last thing we wanted was a new party to saddle itself with that commitment, and there were a lot of commitments which we made for the '83 election which had a sort of passé feel about them already. It was a shame, really. We revived from '83 to '87 the idea of the SDP being the party of ideas. We still did quite well in that election you know; only 2% less. If we'd held our nerve, in 1992 a deal would have been done if the Alliance had kept its position. A great, missed opportunity occurred in 1992, because you had a Labour leader who would have given you proportional representation, and that's where we'd have ended up, we'd have done a deal with Neil Kinnock, even though we could've realistically looked as if we could have talked to John Major. And that's when you get the best deal, is when the two leaders of the bigger parties need the third force. And we would have been a third force. David Steel would have stayed leader of the Liberals, and I'd have been leader of the SDP. Of course the Liberals would have been the stronger party, because we would have not been able to get enough seats, enough members of Parliament; but we'd have still been a broad enough coalition to have been holding the balance in 1992. But these, again, are the 'ifs' of history.

HENNESSY

There's one party leader we haven't talked about, the great figure of the 1980s, Mrs Thatcher. She took rather a shine to you, didn't she? Did she have a shine for you before the Falklands War, when you did rather think alike?

OWEN

I think it was probably the Falklands. We didn't think rather alike; we were totally alike. Both of us knew that if the mistakes that we made in the early stages of that war were not changed, then Britain would be the lesser. That was a war we had to win, actually. There was no nonsense about it. We had to be able to get the Argentinians back off that island. It was a great tribute to our armed services that they did so. And it was a good thing for the SDP that we supported them; but it probably did a great deal of harm, because electorally she was unbeatable after the '82 Falklands war. The '83 election was always going to be won by them.

HENNESSY

Did she call you in for private chats during the war?

OWEN

Yes, she did.

HENNESSY

What did she ask you?

OWEN

Well, it was just on privy counsellor terms, and discuss the situation, sometimes with David Steel. Sometimes we'd just bump into each other and she said, 'Come and have a word?' I remember once, when one of our ships had been very seriously damaged, we lost a lot of people on it, that there was not the slightest hint of hubris or jingoism about her. She was facing a hugely vulnerable situation. I remember once she said, 'We could never bomb the Argentinian airfields on the mainland,' and I went in and I said, 'Be careful, Margaret. If you've got a Super Étendard that has hit the back of one of our aircraft carriers, with *Ark Royal* limping out of the area, and you know they're coming in after you, you'd have to bomb those airfields, you'd have to render them not viable.' She didn't bite back. She took it, you know, she didn't say, 'Nonsense, nonsense!' It troubled her I was saying that. She put up some arguments against it, but I think it was helpful she had a contrary argument put to her on that particular moment.

HENNESSY

That's why the Vulcan did the bombing of the Falklands airfield; it showed that it could reach Argentina. She probably listened to you.

OWEN

Exactly. I think it was a mistake she said that – she was under great pressure to say it, and she probably oughtn't to have said it. But overall, she handled it very well, and the military found her rational, careful, cautious, and she proved to be a good leader in the Falklands.

HENNESSY

What are the ingredients of your admiration for her?

OWEN

Well, I think it was necessary, unfortunately, given where we were over groups like the miners and others, to make changes to the union regulations. They had got too powerful, and they had to be checked. That isn't to deprive them of their rights, their basic rights, their important rights. And I think that was a necessary change, the trade-union reform package which she put together, and the SDP supported it. And there were some elements of markets where we had forgotten that the prosperity of the Victorian period was in our capacity to sell into world markets. I'm a social market man; I believe something some things are social, and you don't have markets in them, like the health service and social provision, and in some things you are a world competitor and you have to have market disciplines, like engineering and building aircraft, and cars and things like that. So I believe in the tough and the tender. There are a certain areas where a market operates, where Britain is ruthlessly out there building markets and building its prosperity; and there are other areas where there are no markets, where you're looking after your own, your disabled, your sick, your mentally ill. And the two are not the same, and pretending they're the same and introducing the market everywhere is wrong, and it is *wrong* that the Labour Party went down that route, and Blair has a lot to answer for. It's not just the Iraq War which went wrong. A lot of these changes in the social-care provisions and the attitudes were basically, fundamentally wrong. The Labour Party should not have gone down that track, and I hope the new leader of the Labour Party gradually puts things back so we can have a passion about some of these things.

HENNESSY

Let's turn to Tony Blair. He tried to get you back into the Labour Party, didn't he? Shortly after becoming leader.

OWEN

Yes, in 1996. I wished him well, we had a very nice conversation, friendly, went on for probably too long for his purposes, because we'd got on to the Euro. And I suddenly realised that this man was totally in favour of us joining the Euro. And the more I talked to him, the less he seemed to know about it. And by this time I'd become absolutely convinced that we shouldn't touch it, that it was flawed intellectually, and in its financial model was flawed, and we shouldn't go near it.

HENNESSY

You became very critical of Tony Blair later, in your book on leaders' psychology and so on.[2] You called him a victim of the hubris syndrome. Do you see him essentially as a tragic figure – all that promise?

OWEN

Well, to be fair, there were things which he did as Prime Minister which were good, and there isn't all together a bad record. It's a tragedy that his conduct since he left office has, I think, made it very difficult for people to be generous enough to him for the good things he did as Prime Minister. It's a terrible ending. But I think he did make a mistake over Iraq, but I made that too. I supported the Iraq war. The actual military invasion went technically quite well; what was terrible was – and I think we'll see when the Chilcot inquiry comes out – that the conduct of the aftermath was appalling, and both Bush and he were so hubristic they thought the war was over. All the experience of the Balkans was that the war isn't over after the peace is signed, the war continues. It's the troops you have on the ground, how you remake peace on the ground when the fighting has stopped, that is absolutely crucial.

HENNESSY

If you'd become Prime Minister, David, how would you have made sure you didn't succumb to the hubris syndrome? Because it quite often goes with the job, particularly if you're there for a long time.

OWEN

Well, I've got a very wonderful wife, who is perfectly prepared to criticise me very seriously, and particularly one-on-one. There is barely a moment when she is not pulling me down, not in the

---

2 David Owen, *The Hubris Syndrome: Bush, Blair and the Intoxication of Power*, (Methuen Publishing, 2012)

nasty sense, but in the sense of quietly saying to me afterwards, 'David, you never gave him enough time to take his viewpoint', or 'You can't speak to people like that'. There have been other people in my life too who've been what I call in the book 'toe-holders'. The wiser you are, you encourage around you people who are strong enough to hold you back, who will challenge your views. I've been extremely lucky in all my jobs in government that I've had civil servants in my private office who are very, very high calibre, who are perfectly prepared to argue with me, and I encouraged it. That's one of the ways that you can stop hubris, is to have people around you who love you but who are strong with you, tough with you, and who are not prepared to let you have your own way. But of course it's better if you've got that control in yourself; but unfortunately, a lot of us get … I'm certainly vulnerable to hubris syndrome, I don't deny it, that's why I write about it. I think it's so important.

HENNESSY

What would an Owen Premiership have looked like? What would you have done on day one? What would have been your style of government?

OWEN

I … don't really want to go down there.

HENNESSY

You must have thought about it, David, come on.

OWEN

Of course you've thought about it, but I don't want to go there, that's … presumptuous. You didn't make it, and don't start believing or thinking that you did. You didn't. Probably the reason you didn't make it was part bad luck – luck plays a huge role in politics – but sometimes, part of it was probably your own deficiencies.

And so you can't ... That's life. I have no regrets. I thoroughly enjoyed my period in politics.

HENNESSY

What trace would you like to leave on history?

OWEN

Who knows what trace one has left, or will leave? I'm not sure. I think one thing is this. That when the politics gets tough and rough, it's perfectly legitimate, proper and right that you should put policies and principles above your party, and that worship of the party is absurd. A party is a vehicle. Be loyal to it, and like it, love it – but don't get into a situation where to leave a political party is treason. You're not a traitor if you take a different political view from your party. Politics is about give and take. I think overall we have a good political system. It's not performing very well at the moment. It's had a bad period, I would say probably since 2003.

HENNESSY

Since the Iraq War.

OWEN

Since the Iraq War, and Afghanistan. These are two defeats. Afghanistan was appallingly handled. We have to learn these lessons. Libya: mistake. I wanted a no-fly zone, it didn't work. I thought the best decision Parliament made in the last five years was to not go into Syria and to allow America to have time to think, and then decide themselves they wouldn't go into Syria. So if Ed Miliband is given not much credit, I hope he'll be given credit for that one at least. That was not going to be a proper military intervention; it was going to be a gesture politics. And now we have this Islamic Republic sitting there in a third to two-thirds of Syria. It was always there. If we had gone in, a military intervention, everybody in the Middle East would be blaming the British, the French and the Americans for going in, and they would say we brought on Isil or Isis. We didn't, it was there already, we weren't going to stop it. Now they have got to have an overall regional solution to this issue, and again we can help them, but we should avoid 1919 Peace Conferences; it was that map which landed Syria in the mess that we're in today.

HENNESSY

If I could grant you one last reform, what would it be?

OWEN

To bring back the National Health Service. The National Health Service came out of the flaws of the private-market system all through the 1920s and 30s, the degradation and the deprivation of not having an overall National Health Service. Bring it back, take out this marketisation. But I am pretty sure the NHS is going to go on deteriorating over the next few years, sadly.

HENNESSY

David Owen, thank you very much indeed.

Nigel Lawson (Lord Lawson of Blaby)

Series 3, Episode 2, first broadcast 20 July 2015

Born 11 March 1932; **Educated** Westminster School; Christ Church, Oxford

MP (Conservative) Blaby 1974–1992

Financial Secretary to the Treasury, 1979–81; Secretary of State for Energy, 1981–83; Chancellor of the Exchequer, 1983–89

Autobiography *The View from No 11*, 1992; rev. edition as *Memoirs of a Tory Radical*, 2010

HENNESSY

With me today is Nigel Lawson, Lord Lawson of Blaby, a self-proclaimed Tory radical, and one of only a handful of post-war Chancellors of the Exchequer who, during the Premiership of Margaret Thatcher, truly changed the nature of Britain's political economy with his tax reforms. Nigel, welcome.

LAWSON

Thank you very much, Peter.

HENNESSY

Tell me about your home background: was it a political family in north London, in Hampstead?

LAWSON

No, not at all political. Indeed, I didn't intend to go into politics myself. It was a very conventional, comfortably-off, middle-class home.

HENNESSY

Was it a religious family?

LAWSON

Not at all.

HENNESSY

Slightly impertinent question, but are you a religious person?

LAWSON

No, I'm not. I used to think about these things and didn't come to any conclusion. When I became an undergraduate at Oxford, reading mainly philosophy – but it wasn't mainly because of that – I thought about it very hard, and I used to discuss these things very deeply with a number of my Catholic friends in particular. And I came to the conclusion that I couldn't believe in God; and I used to call myself an agnostic, but then later on I thought, 'Well that's pretty gutless; if you're an atheist, you should call yourself an atheist'. So I've been an atheist ever since, and that's a long time ago, that was since I went up to Oxford in 1951; and I've seen no reason whatsoever to change my view. But I'm not an aggressive atheist because I've had so many religious friends who are good people, and the last thing I want to do is offend them.

HENNESSY

Was Oxford a fairly exotic experience? You'd been at Westminster School in London, and I think you got a scholarship in Mathematics and changed to PPE, but concentrated on the linguistic analysis – pretty austere stuff – but did you have a kind of lotus-eating existence on the side, if I can put it like that?

LAWSON

Oh yes, I spent most of my time going to parties. Indeed, I was warned by one of my tutors, a particularly silly man, that if I didn't stop going to parties I would only get a Third for my degree. And I didn't take any notice of him. No, the party life was great.

HENNESSY

Napoleon had this dictum that if you want to understand a man or woman in authority, as you were to be later, think of the world as it was when they were 20. And if it works in your case, it may not, it was the gradual ending of austerity, the Attlee government was just over, Churchill setting the people free and all that. Did you absorb political instincts and views at that time? Was that part of your formation at Oxford, having been apolitical at home?

LAWSON

Yes, I was very critical. The first government that I was aware of, really, was the post-war Labour government, the Attlee government of 1945. And I could see that socialism didn't work.

HENNESSY

Which bits in particular?

LAWSON

The economy was a disaster. But also it was clear to me that they had no understanding of human nature, and that they were trying to change human beings in a way that suited their ideas, that were no doubt very high-minded – but you can't change human beings, at least, very rarely. Some people think about progress, and there is a lot of progress, largely in technology; but I don't think there has been any progress whatever in human nature.

HENNESSY

That's rather a bleak analysis, Nigel.

HENNESSY

No it isn't, human nature has its good and its bad aspects, but there is absolutely no progress in human nature. People today are not any better than people in the past, but the technology is better, so we live more comfortable lives.

HENNESSY

Did you absorb what used to be called the post-war consensus? The Churchill government, Rab Butler being particularly influential, accepted the welfare-state aspect of the post-1945 settlement, and many of the nationalisations. So there was a very powerful relative consensus, I think one would call it, in the early '50s, between the two front benches. Were you Keynesian, were you welfare-state-ish? Even though your view of human nature was not perhaps that of Stafford Cripps, who was a saintly figure?

LAWSON

I was never welfare-stateish. I was brought up, as everyone was at that time, with Keynesian economics, maybe particularly so in my case because my economics tutor, Roy Harrod, was a great disciple of Keynes, and indeed wrote the first biography of Keynes. And he thought Keynes was a very great man, and I liked Roy a lot; but I have a naturally sceptical mind, and therefore I never did take when I was young whatever my tutors told me, I thought, I'll reserve judgement. That was the only economics I knew at the time. And then time passed, and it was clear that the Keynesian policies being pursued by that time by the governments of both parties were not outstandingly successful. And this was a very sad thing for this country. We'd won the war, and we thought we could be successful in the peace after the war, and we were markedly unsuccessful in the economic sphere, and it was a great concern.

HENNESSY

We had growth and we had full employment in the '50s, however
...

LAWSON

It began well but it rapidly went south at the start of the '60s, which were a very bad time.

HENNESSY

So it's the '60s when you began to realise that there may be some flaws in all this?

LAWSON

That's right.

HENNESSY

In a very interesting lecture in 1988 at the Centre for Policy Studies, 'The Tide of Ideas From Attlee to Thatcher', you talk about the two great weather systems in post-war British politics: the Attleean settlement – the mixed economy, welfare state – and Mrs Thatcher's rolling back the state, and to some degree the welfare state, though never really touching the health service. Do you think those are still the great weather-maker premierships of our post-war politics?

LAWSON

Yes I do. It is quite clear that the Attleeite settlement long out-lived the Attlee government, and the broad lines of that were largely followed by the subsequent Conservative government, by Winston Churchill, who was not particularly happy with it, but he was only a shadow of his former self when he was the post-war Prime Minister. But the rest of the Conservative government accepted this as a change because there had been this theory, this belief, that somehow the Depression of the 1930s had destroyed the old idea of the capitalist free-enterprise economy, and indeed the descent into depression in the 1930s was a terrible experience. But I think the analysis of *why* it happened was wrong; still, that was the conventional analysis, and it was on that basis that the Attleeite settlement wasn't really rejected at all by the Conservative Party and consecutive Conservative governments. And it was not until Margaret Thatcher came into office in 1979 that a radical change was introduced, and it *was* a radical change. And the subsequent Labour government in effect endorsed that; Tony Blair basically endorsed it. And so it has survived in the way that for a long time the Attleeite settlement survived. These are the two great weather-changers, to use your expression, Peter, in post-war British politics.

HENNESSY

It intrigues me, what you just said, because one of your strong characteristics, Nigel, if I may put it this way, is that you cannot see a consensus without wanting to biff it; you don't like going with the tide of ideas if you think that people are getting carried away with an orthodoxy. And yet your time as Mrs Thatcher's Chancellor, particularly those tax changes which have been only partially reversed, means that you're one of the architects of the current consensus.

LAWSON

But that's what I sought to be. I was not anti-consensus, Margaret was. Margaret hated the idea of consensus *in itself*. I just hated the idea of the consensus we'd had before, which clearly was mistaken. No, I did hope that there would be a consensus around what you might call Thatcherite policies. I very much hoped that. Because after all, when you're in government you are working very, very hard, and you're trying to achieve something, but you're not trying to achieve something just for your term of office, you're trying to achieve something which will endure after you're out of office because everyone comes out of office sooner or later, and sometimes sooner rather than later. And so I was very anxious that our approach to economic policy in particular would endure, but also it was within a wider framework of understanding what a government is about and what a free country is about. And indeed, one of the things I was always keen to do, like in the privatisation programme, was to entrench the privatisations by having the widest possible spread of shareholdings, so that it made it much harder for a subsequent government to reverse it.

HENNESSY

So I must see you now as Nigel the consensualist.

LAWSON

Absolutely.

HENNESSY

There's another element in your Conservatism, which I trace a long way back, certainly reading your memoirs, which is patriotism, good old-fashioned patriotism.

LAWSON

Yes.

HENNESSY

And I remember you expressed it very vividly once, when we were talking about the pride, the legitimate pride, you hold in being one of the few national servicemen in the Royal Navy to command your own vessel.

LAWSON

Yes, I was lucky.

HENNESSY

The motor-torpedo boat named …?

LAWSON

Gay Charger.

HENNESSY

How terrific.

LAWSON

But 'gay' in those days meant something different from what it means today.

HENNESSY

Certainly in the Royal Navy. [*They laugh*]

HENNESSY

You left Oxford and went into journalism – why was that?

LAWSON

Because I was always interested, like you, in public affairs. And I felt that I would enjoy that more than anything else. I also, I suppose – I don't want to sound pompous or priggish – but I always felt that I would like to do something for the public good, and since I can't do anything creative or artistic for the public good, the one thing I could do was maybe contribute to public affairs.

HENNESSY

And was the worm of political ambition at work already as well?

LAWSON

No, I didn't particularly want to enter politics. I thought my contribution to public affairs could be the best done by writing, critical writing; and indeed, I also, I think, had the prejudice which is frequent among the young in general, and among young journalists in particular, that politicians are a disreputable lot of people. And indeed I think the only thing which really, completely, got rid of that feeling for me – although as I'd been a journalist and got to meet them and I realised there were all sorts, and there are some extremely decent people – was working for Alec Home, who was a man of such complete integrity and he had also done well in politics. The integrity had not prevented him getting to the top – and so then I took a different view of politics and politicians.

HENNESSY

Were you for Mrs Thatcher from the beginning?

LAWSON

I was, really, yes; and this was not just because of her political views, but her personal qualities. I didn't know her, really, very well. I came across her slightly and she had impressed me, when I was asked to write the 1974 manifesto – I had at that time decided that I would like to go into politics, and therefore I was working for the Conservative Party, and they asked me. There was a draft manifesto already in existence, because they prepare for these things, but it had been written a long time ago, and the world had changed, and politics had changed so much, that it had to be completely redone afresh. And so one of the first things I did was to write to every member of the Cabinet, and I said, 'I would like you to let me have a draft of what you would like to see in your area of policy in the manifesto.' And they all sent me things which had clearly been written by their officials, they were absolutely useless. The one person who had written her own, clearly, was the chapter I was sent on education policy; Margaret was at that time Secretary of State for Education, and it was clearly written by her. Indeed, there were crossings out, and changes in her own hand. And it was quite different from what all the others had sent me. I had never met her then; that made an impression on me.

HENNESSY

And she becomes Prime Minister in '79 and you go to the Treasury as Financial Secretary. How would you sum up her style as Prime Minister? As manager of Cabinet, for example.

LAWSON

She certainly didn't see herself as just a sort of non-executive Chairman. She had this engaging habit of summing up at the beginning, and then seeing if anybody had the guts to challenge her summing up. That was how she approached it. She also, sometimes, didn't know what she wanted. She didn't always know what she wanted. And when she didn't know what she wanted, the meetings could go on and on and on, going round and round and round. And that was particularly true in Cabinet committees. And so I had to suggest to her that I would have, in-between meetings with the committee, a committee of my own to try and make progress, because otherwise we were going to go round and round for ever. But she was very strong, she had very strong views. She liked an argument, and the people who got bullied by her, like Geoffrey Howe, they never argued with her, that was the problem. I mean, he would stubbornly persist with his own views, but he would never actually argue. She loved an argument; obviously, she wanted to win every argument. But she didn't just want, as it was popularly known, a Cabinet of 'Yes Men'. It was helpful to me because, although she and I had very different personalities and characters, we were at one on a number of ideas. I came into Parliament late in life, I was over 40 before I became a Member of Parliament, and I'd been writing all the time; so my ideas on the need to break away completely from the old failed consensus – it was not just negative, I had a clear idea of what we needed to do – chimed very well with what she'd come to think and believe.

HENNESSY

As an old journalist, you were quite a connoisseur of watching her press operation, weren't you. Her press secretary, Bernard Ingham, would do the cuttings, leading with *The Sun.*

LAWSON

Yes.

HENNESSY

Can you describe how you rumbled that particular operation? Because it needed a journalist's eye to see what was going on.

LAWSON

She didn't read the newspapers, except on the weekend. She relied entirely on Bernard Ingham's press summary, and Bernard Ingham's press summary was delivered not only to Number 10 but to Number 11 as well; so I didn't have to be very clever to know what he was feeding her with. And he would always lead with *The Sun,* and there was a curious circularity about his press summaries, because he would have been the person who'd told *The Sun* what to write in the first place. So [*laughs*] all that was happening was that he would then say, 'Prime Minister, very important, this is what *The Sun* has to say, and they are most closely in touch with the people of this country, as you know.'

HENNESSY

So she thought she had a unique access to the minds of the British people because of this particular operation?

LAWSON

Absolutely, yes.

HENNESSY

Very clever. Not many people rumbled that at the time.

LAWSON

I don't think so.

HENNESSY

No. Going back to the Keynesian orthodoxy that you were instrumental in puncturing, if I can put it that way – how tough was it to turn around that orthodoxy?

LAWSON

It would have been very tough but for one thing, and that was that the experiences of the Labour government in the 1970s, before we came into office in 1979, had been so bad that the Treasury officials – for whom I have a very high regard, and I couldn't have done what I did without them – but those officials were, fortunately, completely demoralised. They were shell-shocked. They were shattered, particularly after the experience when the British government had to go cap-in-hand to the IMF.

HENNESSY

In 1976.

LAWSON

In 1976, the first industrialised country that had ever done that. And that was a humiliation. So they didn't believe at all in what we said we were going to do – maybe one or two did, but the majority of the mandarinate in the Treasury didn't – but they had nothing else to offer, and they were as I say completely demoralised and shell shocked, so we were able to have our way with much less difficulty than what would otherwise have been the case.

HENNESSY

Did you expect with the set of policies that the first Thatcher government brought in – loosely labelled Monetarism which is an inadequate label, but there it is, that's what it was called – would produce quite such high unemployment?

LAWSON

No, we never expected that to happen. But what it demonstrated, of course, was the huge inefficiency in so much of British industry, worst of all in the nationalised sector, but also in other large companies. There was huge over-manning in the nationalised industries, and in most large corporations. When there was a clear financial discipline applied, and the government was no longer going to be a soft touch, there was a shake-out of the over-manning, so unemployment rose to a very high level, which was very distressing, we didn't want it. But it was a necessary part of the correction. We weren't going to be deterred from pursuing these policies because of the high level of unemployment, which governments in the past, when they tentatively tried, on the few occasions they had tried what we were doing, were so terrified by that they always thought that they could not go ahead; and of course it all worked out very well, and unemployment eventually came down. But it took a long time, and it required a lot of nerve, which is a great credit to Margaret Thatcher, again.

HENNESSY

Can we turn now to your refashioning of the political economy? I think economic historians will see it probably in two parts: liberalising the City, the 'Big Bang'[1], and then later the tax changes, the standard rate and the highest rate and so on. Did you have an idea in your head of a new political economy, in the way that Mr Gladstone would have had in the 19th century?

LAWSON

Oh yes, there was certainly a need for deregulation. Not solely the

---

1 The deregulation of financial markets in 1986

City. The deregulation went across the board. The fact was that we had two problems with the economy, stemming from the semi-socialist way in which it was organised. What it meant was that not only did we have a union movement which was harmful, but that management on the whole was lousy. Because if you were a businessman you were so hamstrung by regulations of one kind or another that you decided that the best use of your time was to lobby the government for more favours – regulation which might put your competitors out of business rather than you, or permission to do this or permission to do that. And that is the death of good management. So we were suffering not merely from a bad union movement, but rotten management. So a real change had to be introduced, and I was determined to do it. On banking and the Big Bang, incidentally, I was very concerned that the quality of the necessary regulation for the banks, that is to say prudential regulation, was inadequate; and I introduced what became the Banking Act of 1987, which greatly increased the quality of banking supervision and banking regulation. Unfortunately, when Gordon Brown took over in 1997, he first of all neutered it and then abolished it, and put in its place a totally ineffective and dysfunctional form of bank supervision and bank regulation. And it is possible, who knows, that if the system that I put in place had persisted, we would not have had quite such a bad experience in 2008.

HENNESSY

So there's the privatisation of the nationalised industries, which we've talked about, there's the Big Bang, and then there's the tax changes in 1988, which probably will be seen as your greatest legacy.

LAWSON

Well, I'm very happy to have any legacy at all. But politics moves on. Privatisation was a very radical policy. It had never been done.

There had been progressive episodes of nationalisation, but when the Conservatives got in, they never unwound them. So nationalisation grew and grew. The idea that you could somehow go back from state ownership to private ownership – that had never been tried at all, and had never been tried anywhere in the world. And we were the pioneers in this country, and it was subsequently followed all over the world, first of all in the Western world, and then subsequently in the countries which had escaped from the Soviet Union, the Soviet Empire, rather. And they went in for privatisation. And indeed it was this country which not only gave the policy to the rest of the world, but it gave the word 'privatisation', which is now used in every language under the sun.

HENNESSY

Perhaps your one big failure, when historians look back, will be the Poll Tax, because I think you could have killed the Poll Tax. I think in your memoir, you almost say that if you'd turned up to a meeting at Chequers, and made the Treasury's case against it, you might have stopped it.

LAWSON

I don't think so. She was determined to do it, and I was the only opponent. It was a big mistake, you're quite right, not to be at that meeting, which was the first collective discussion of it. But I don't think it would have made any difference. I fought it very hard. The problem was that it was local taxation. And the Chancellor of the Exchequer's writ runs as far as national taxation is concerned, and Margaret couldn't have done anything in the field of national taxation which I disagreed with. She could not have done that. But local government taxation is a different matter. I argued with her, first of all in private, very strongly that this would be a disaster; when the Cabinet committee was discussing it I wrote the most hostile memorandum because the Treasury has the right to put forward a Cabinet paper on any legislation, uniquely the Treasury, on anybody else's legislation. And I put it in the paper, which was the most hostile paper that I ever put into Cabinet. And so she knew fully my view and so did all my colleagues, but none of them were prepared to stand up and be counted. And I also signalled my opposition, but it was perhaps too subtle, by the fact that when the Bill came forward I was asked as Chancellor to put my name on it because there'd never been a tax Bill of any kind that didn't have the Chancellor's name on it. And I refused to do so. But nobody picked it up – the press are very dozy and very lazy.

HENNESSY

You should have leaked it.

LAWSON

I was never a leaker.

HENNESSY

No, you weren't.

LAWSON

I was never a leaker. I was opposed to leaking. I didn't want to leaked against, and therefore I felt it would be wrong for me to leak. But my opposition was well known. Margaret knew – and indeed, she used to see journalists and say, 'I've seen off Nigel.' You know there was no secret of it. So I don't think it is right, Peter, to say I didn't fight it.

HENNESSY

Relationships were souring, I suspect, by this time with Mrs Thatcher generally. One of the most striking things in your memoir is when you say how you went to see the Queen to brief her on the '89 budget and said, 'I can only say this to you privately because you won't leak, you don't leak. This will be my last budget, it's all becoming impossible.'

LAWSON

At the end it did. I mean I had a number of very good years with her, and I admire her enormously. She was a great Prime Minister, there's no two ways about it. I don't think she was as great in her latter years as she was earlier on, but we were very, very close, fighting shoulder-to-shoulder, both in opposition and then in government for many years. And it only went sour at the end.

HENNESSY

What was the reason for it? There must have been multiple reasons, I suppose ...

LAWSON

I suppose so. I think ... that the fact that I was frequently critical – I always had expressed myself, I hope, in an acceptable way but often in a critical way, when we were discussing things. If I thought that she was mistaken I think that she had earlier on quite welcomed it, she liked argument, and she did see herself during the earlier years as the captain of a team. At some point, and these things are gradual, they don't happen suddenly, she saw her self less and less as a team player, and more and more as the great leader, and the team were really surplus to requirements. And so that changed her relationship, not just with me but her relationship with her Cabinet colleagues altogether, I think, changed. And I think that the Poll Tax – which is a huge political misjudgement, and I think most people, if they weren't architects of the Poll Tax, recognise that now – was a misjudgement she would not have made in the early years. She would have been far too cautious. She became – to use the word said to me by a Permanent Secretary – she became careless. And in the early years she was *anything* but careless, she was extremely careful. She was radical, but she was not careless.

HENNESSY

And the last straw was the Alan Walters business, her personal economic adviser at Number 10, who you thought, I think, was having too much say.

LAWSON

No, it was not that he was having too much say. I'm always happy to debate anything. But he was not saying it just in private, he was saying it publicly. And that is unacceptable for an adviser to be doing that, and it is particularly unacceptable in this area, because when the financial markets don't understand what the policy is, because they have two different policies coming at them, one ostensibly the Prime Minister's policy because it's from the Prime Minister's special adviser, and the other from the Chancellor, then they don't know what to believe. And so this complete failure to have the financial markets on our side, which we had had in the past, makes the conduct of economic policy very, very much harder. And so I said to her, 'Look, you know, this is an impossible situation. Either Alan has to go or I will go, and I will quite understand it if you want me to go, because you're the Prime Minister and he is your adviser.' And she said, 'Oh no, I don't want you to go, you mustn't go, you mustn't go.' And she thought I was bluffing. She thought that it was a bluff. But you know, I didn't make that statement in private without having thought it through, and you don't do that unless you are prepared to go if the thing goes against you. The irony is that the hullaballoo in the markets in the wake of my resignation was so great that he had to go as well.

HENNESSY

And just over a year later, she was gone too.

LAWSON

And she was gone too. I don't think it was because of that, but I don't think that helped.

HENNESSY

Economic historians looking back might say that one of the paradoxes of your time in the Treasury was that in the end it created what in the shorthand was known as the Lawson Boom. That here were you, who kept your nerve and so on in the early 80s despite the high unemployment and all the rest of it, but you let it rip, a bit, towards the end.

LAWSON

No, I didn't let it rip; it ripped. I actually secured a budget surplus, which the present Chancellor, whom I have a high regard for, would give his eyeteeth for. I eliminated the deficit and got a surplus. I didn't let things rip. I think that in so far as I did make a mistake, I perhaps contributed to a mood of overconfidence by making confident speeches, because the conduct of economic policy is not science. There is a kind of scientific dimension to it, but there also, perhaps even more important, a psychological dimension to it; and if I got anything wrong, which I probably did, it was not the economics, it was the psychology. Actually Keynes explained the economic cycle entirely in terms of psychological mood swings.

HENNESSY

Animal spirits and all that.

LAWSON

Well, more than that. In those days there was no such thing as consumer credit except for the wealthy, the borrowing was all done really by business, borrowing to invest; if you're not investing, you don't need to borrow. So it was this cycle between business being extremely optimistic about the future and so borrowing an awful lot in order to invest for the future, in plant and machinery and so on, and then suddenly getting worried they've done too much, and so they get unconfident, they don't borrow any more, indeed they may repay any borrowing if they can. And that is what, in Keynes's analysis, determines the economic cycle: it's mood swings, basically psychology. And to the extent that I got something wrong, I think that I should have been making rather bearish speeches towards the end instead of saying, 'Look how well the economy's doing.' But it's natural when the economy *is* doing well for ministers to say, look how well it's doing. I'm not the first minister to have done that. [*Laughs*]

HENNESSY

Nigel, you've remained a man of causes, right through the years, since you left high office, left the Treasury. One of them is global warming. It's very interesting, reading the book you wrote on it, I think, in 2008 …

LAWSON

Right.

HENNESSY

… *An Appeal to Reason.* Your natural scepticism is there, which we've talked about. But you've always talked about the need for realism in politics, and indeed human nature doesn't change and all the rest of it, you're very eloquent about that. But an overwhelming proportion of the scientific community do think something very serious is happening that we can't ignore, and that adaptation – which human kind always goes in for anyway – won't be enough, that you need mitigation. But you have you come out very strongly against that, and some people would say – is your view evidence-based policy or is it policy-based evidence?

LAWSON

No, the conventional wisdom is policy-based evidence. I am on the evidence-based policy side. You talk about the overwhelming majority of scientists. That is not true; there may be a majority, but some of the best scientists in the world – including, for example,

Freeman Dyson, of Princeton, who is widely regarded as the great-est living physicist – is on the academic advisory council of my think-tank, and I have other great scientists.

HENNESSY

Having said that, Nigel, there's a great many very senior scientists who have been very concerned about this increasingly for a very long time, and you're implying that they're suffering from a Grand Delusion, with a capital G and a capital D.

LAWSON

Well, they're not economists. And there are three dimensions, four dimensions really, to the global-warming issue, which is one of the reasons why I was attracted to it: there's the scientific, there's the economic – what policies make economic sense, which are cost-effective and so on; and there's the political dimension – can you get a global agreement, and if you can't get a global agreement, what sense is there in the United Kingdom going ahead when we're responsible for less than 2% of global carbon emissions; and then there's the ethical dimension, which I think I've come to feel most strongly about. The only reason we use fossil fuels is that they are by far and away the cheapest and most reliable source of energy. That may not always be the case. But it is the case now, and it will be for the foreseeable future. That's why we use them. And this has a huge bearing on the alleviation of poverty, which is par-ticularly important in the developing world, although obviously there are pockets of poverty in the developed world as well. And therefore you want to get people out of poverty, and you need to use the cheapest and most reliable form of energy. And to say that you don't give a damn about the people who are alive today, your-self, your children, and in my case, my grandchildren, but that for people hundreds of years hence, people who will in any case because of economic growth be considerably richer than those alive today, in order *possibly* to be helpful to them, you've got to do harm to the people and the poor people alive today – that strikes me as profoundly unethical.

HENNESSY

You've got another great cause as well, which is Europe, the European Union. Is it true, by the way, that when you were asked why you live such a high proportion of the year in France, you replied, 'Because I like to live outside the European Union'?

LAWSON

I did say that, but that was something of a joke; but the point was – it's not entirely a joke – the point was that the European Union legislation, which is terribly bureaucratic and so on, is taken much more seriously in this country than it is in France. But no, France is my home, I love France, and far from being anti-European, I love France, and I live there out of choice. But one must never make the mistake of confusing Europe with the European Union.

HENNESSY

Nigel, what do you think history will remember you for? What trace will you leave on history, your public and political life?

LAWSON

I don't know. You said earlier on that maybe it's the tax reforms which will endure; and I think they were tremendously important, and I think that to a considerable extent, not totally, they have outlived my time in office. And the approach to taxation, which sounds small, but it affects everybody, and has a considerable bearing on the success of the economy, and it has influences overseas. But I'd like to think there was more than that, but what it is, I wouldn't know. You know I think that's for historians like you; it's not for humble people like me to define what posterity will say.

HENNESSY

I should say you're smiling at this point. [*Nigel laughs*]

LAWSON

But I do think that you refer to me, because I refer to myself, as a Tory radical, and I do think that's a pretty good combination, Toryism and radicalism.

HENNESSY

Do you have one great regret in your public and political life?

LAWSON

Well, my regret … my regret is clear. My regret is that circumstances arose in which I felt I had no alternative but to resign.

HENNESSY

In 1989 …

LAWSON

In 1989. I regret that those circumstances arose. But if they had not arisen, I would not have resigned; and equally, if they had arisen at a later date, I would have resigned. It was not that I think that my reaction to the state of affairs in which I found myself was a mistaken one. It wasn't an easy one, I thought long and hard about it, and the arguments were balanced on each side – but what I really regret is that that state of affairs arose in the first place.

HENNESSY

If I could give you one last reform, what would it be? What would you want?

LAWSON

Well I think two reforms I would like relate to the two main causes which I have been fighting now, even in my great old age, which you've mentioned, although there is a third.

HENNESSY

So that's Climate Change and Europe, but a third one?

LAWSON

The third one is banking. I think the lessons of the banking melt-down, and the appalling bad behaviour of the bankers, which led to the meltdown in 2008 – they've not been sufficiently learned. OK, there were certainly mistaken policies, and the Labour government's abandonment of the stronger supervision that I put in place was a huge error. But there's no getting away – the bankers behaved very badly, and this has to do with the culture of banking. And I firmly believe that we need to have a complete separation between what used to be known as High Street Banking, which has to be terribly prudent, must be prudent, and investment banking, which used to be known as merchant banking, which is exciting and creative and all that, and that's all very well and good, but it's anything but prudent. If you have the two things together, if the culture of imprudence and risk-taking – particularly because banks know at the back of their minds that if the risk goes sour the taxpayer will bail them out – if that infects the main body of banking, the joint-stock banking, and destroys the prudence there, we're in deep trouble. We're in even deeper trouble, because, of course, it is the joint-stock banks, which have the deposits from the public, and so those are at risk, and ultimately the taxpayer stands behind them. So I believe you need a complete separation. The government, who set up the Vickers Commission, which was asked to look into this, the government has accepted the logic but not the conclusion. They've accepted that there must be a ring-fence between high-street banking and investment banking; that's never been done anywhere in the world, for a very good reason: I don't think it's workable. You have to have a separation. So that's one reform that I would like to see. The other two are the repeal of the Climate Change Act and Britain's exit from the European Union.

HENNESSY

You're as radical as ever. Nigel Lawson, thank you very much.

LAWSON

Thank you, Peter.

Clare Short

Series 3, Episode 3, 27 July 2015

Born 15 February 1946; **Educated** St Paul's Grammar School,
Birmingham; Keele University; Leeds University.

MP (Labour) Birmingham, Ladywood 1983–
2010 (Independent, 2006–10).

Secretary of State for International Development, 1997–2003.

Autobiography *An Honourable Deception?*, 2004

HENNESSY

With me today is Clare Short, a politician of often outspoken
passion and individuality. Not always at ease with the disciplines
of party politics or collective Cabinet responsibility, she first
stayed then resigned from the Blair Cabinet over the invasion of
Iraq. Clare, welcome.

SHORT

Thank you.

HENNESSY

Tell me about your early life. I think your political values are very
much embedded in your family. And you were born the second of
seven children in a Catholic family; your father was originally a
teacher in Crossmaglen …

SHORT

He came from Crossmaglen, but he came to London to study as a teacher. I think he was meant to be a priest if he'd stayed in Northern Ireland. And then he taught in Britain.

HENNESSY

So it's a classic Catholic, religious family with a lot of Irish influence in it? In the early '50s …

SHORT

That's right. My Catholic childhood is a deep part of who I am; the belief that you have to try and be truthful and care for people and be fair, and the poor should be looked after. And of course later I gave up the church, because of ridiculous teachings on contraception and all the rest; but that core of me comes from that childhood, and that best side of Catholicism, I would say.

HENNESSY

So it's still there, deep within you …

SHORT

In fact I love Pope Francis; [*laughing*] if only he'd been around a lot earlier.

HENNESSY

Your father had a strong sense of injustice about the treatment of Ireland by British governments over the years; that's another part of your formation.

SHORT

Indeed; and that led to a belief that the British Empire wasn't a good thing, and a sort of sense of solidarity with Africa and Asia in so on. We weren't hectored at; these were just deep values that trickled through the family, and if you met my sisters and brothers, we're all different, but we've all got this core in us of similar values.

HENNESSY

I think these core values erupted, if that's the right word, at the time of the Suez Crisis, when you were only 10. I think you took a different view in the playground about the invasion of Egypt from some of the other school kids.

SHORT

That's right. This is St Francis Catholic Primary School in Birmingham Handsworth, and the children are singing, 'We'll throw Nasser in the Suez Canal!', which must have been going around. And I got them all together and said, 'Listen, that's wrong. This canal is in Egypt, and if they want to take control of it they're entitled to their canal. You shouldn't sing that song.'

HENNESSY

That was very precocious, and somewhat brave, wasn't it?

SHORT

Well, I don't think it was brave really, they just listened to me. I don't know if they carried on singing it when I wasn't there! I suppose it was precocious but I still think it.

HENNESSY

You went to grammar school in Birmingham; did you flourish there? Were you one of those classic products of the 1944 Education Act who went up the ladders of opportunity that simply weren't there for previous generations? Did you feel that at the time?

SHORT

My mother went there and had to leave early because my granny had a difficult pregnancy with her youngest child. So I knew that, and I'd had aunts who went there; it's the girls' Catholic grammar school in Birmingham. I flourished, I liked it, but I got lots of order marks. I was often the elected prefect but I had to write down the order marks, and sometimes mine were more than anyone else's.

HENNESSY

Order marks being tickings-off ...

SHORT

Yes: three and you have to stay in half an hour and write out lines or something. They put us into an A Form and then two alphabetical B Forms, and I was in the A Form, and I'd do reasonably well and work reasonably hard and have a lot of fun and play a lot of netball. And then, when I came to 16, I said to my dad, 'I don't want to stay at school any more.' And he arranged for me to do my A-levels in a local FE college. So I thrived, but I wasn't a sort of goody-goody. But I enjoyed it.

HENNESSY

It seems to me you're a natural-born member of the awkward squad ...

SHORT

Yes, but I don't hate anyone, I never have. I used to get into trouble for talking too much, we used to bag seats at the back of the classroom, and they'd always bring me to the front in the end. I was just a bit exuberant, and a bit un-deferential, but not completely uncooperative. Which I think I'm probably still.

HENNESSY

You did Politics at Leeds – were you active in the Student Union, with Jack Straw? I think he was president of the Student Union at the time.

SHORT

No, I wasn't active in the Student Union. That was the time of Enoch Powell and those sort of racist politicians, and there were demonstrations against them. They'd come and speak and I'd go to those meetings. I sometimes thought the way the protests went was a bit silly. There was a sit-in at Leeds, and I can remember Jack standing on a table reading out telegrams in support of the sit-in, and it was a silly sit-in. There was cause for it in other parts of the country, with files being kept on students; it was purely imitative in Leeds. So Jack Straw, the sensible man, was a bit on the silly side then, [*laughing*] from my 19-year-old point of view.

SHORT

Do you think because of having a political formation at home, you weren't going to succumb to what Nye Bevan would have called in a different context 'emotional spasms' of the late-adolescent kind?

SHORT

I think I was a bit too grown up for some of the silly side of student politics. I joined the local Labour Party in Chapeltown, the 1970 election. We really thought that, Keith Joseph[1], we were going to defeat him. And of course we didn't. [*Laughs*]

HENNESSY

Why on earth did you join the Civil Service, with these characteristics that you describe so vividly? You're not a natural fit; you weren't a sort of Permanent Secretary in the making, were you?

SHORT

No … But there is a serious side to me. You know, I did my work at university, I read the books, I still refer back to some of what

---

1 Conservative MP for Leeds North East and later Margaret Thatcher's Industry Secretary and Education Secretary

I learned. There's another side of me, I'm not just a sort of troublesome person, I think. And why I took the exams for the Civil Service, which was the old 'privileged entry' system, was that I really wanted to have a look at the British Establishment at work.

HENNESSY

Did you find it? Did you find that elusive thing called the British Establishment?

SHORT

I did. And I found that some sides of it were very honourable and decent – public servants helping to run good constitutional arrangements. I mean, they were a bit conservative for my view, but I came to respect them.

HENNESSY

That's very interesting. Were you tempted to join the British Establishment? Not that there's a form you can fill in.

SHORT

I could have stayed; I got promoted to the next rank, and so on. But I loved the policy stuff and, you know, when I was Private Secretary to a Minister I was in the Home Office, which did Northern Ireland then, and prisons and police and so on. But when I went with my ministers to the House of Commons, and gave them the pieces of paper telling them what to say, I thought, if I were there I could *do* the policy, and be myself, and speak my mind. So it was when I saw politicians at work and experienced the tantalising interest of getting better policy that I decided I wanted to get into politics in order to do policy with my own perspective and views.

HENNESSY

I think you fell in love with one of your Ministers.

SHORT

Well, I married Alex, yes indeed, that's right. My previous one was Mark Carlisle. We got on fine but I didn't fall in love with him. [*Laughs*]

HENNESSY

Alex Lyon is remembered very warmly by people who knew him. What influence did he have on you, apart from the fact that you fell in love? Did he teach you anything about politics? What were his special insights?

SHORT

He was a very committed Methodist, and he was very principled and decent. We had this massive backlog of immigration cases with divided families, and he worked incredibly hard trying to reunite divided families. This was before DNA-testing came along and showed that, sure enough, they were real families. The system had become quite cruel in separating families. And I admired his work and his principled-ness. And that might have influenced me – I think, *did* – to think you can, with honour, serve in politics and become a minister, and do good and be a decent person.

HENNESSY

Not the view that the public has of the political class these days; but you saw the very best of the public-service political tradition, as you've just described it.

SHORT

Indeed, though I was there in the two elections in 1974 in the private office and so on; so I saw deep contention in politics. I do think, with the public, that things have deteriorated. It's a complex thing to explain, but I think it has to do with leading figures having to be media people, and the media being the dominant discourse. As less and less people read the press, it becomes more and more powerful, it's a very odd thing. So long-term thinking, principled positions, all go out of the window for tomorrow's headline, and nothing is thought through. So there's been a grave deterioration, it seems to me, and we need to think more about why it's happened, and how we could correct it.

HENNESSY

You come into Parliament in 1983, representing the area of Birmingham in which you grew up; that must have been rather an exquisite pleasure, and also, presumably, it creates an extra-special bond.

SHORT

I think that's right. It is a great pleasure, you know, 'That's where my granny lived, that's where I went to school, that's the church where I was baptised, made my first Communion', da dee da. I still do love the place and feel a lot of respect for the people. And although we were of Irish origin but born in Birmingham – my mother was Potato Famine Irish – the new migrants that became in the end the predominant population I saw as on the same journey as we had been. Same people from different continents, maybe different religions, but same story. So I felt very close, and identified with my constituents. And I had hours-long advice bureaus, and I felt honoured the way people trusted me, and I learned a lot from what was hurting them about what was wrong. It was good, I enjoyed it.

HENNESSY

You came in when Mrs Thatcher was at her zenith as Prime Minister. Even though your politics were and remain, I'm sure, very, very different, was there a little bit of you that was terribly pleased there was a woman Prime Minister?

SHORT

No, not a little, little bit. I mean, unemployment in my constituency went shooting up, we had terrible riots, and there was the miners' strike. I always saw Scargill and her as kind of similar characters, but I think a decent government would have tried to bring it to an end more quickly. And no, I didn't respect her, I'm afraid, at all.

HENNESSY

Do you think she respected you? She liked women of strong opinions, didn't she?

SHORT

I was a blip, probably, on her consciousness. She used to say hello in the corridor, kind of thing, but I was a young, new backbench MP on the other side. I don't suppose she thought much about me.

HENNESSY

You'd seen the Commons in operation as a civil servant in the in the officials' box in the Chamber, and I'm sure you had a very considerable feel for the place; but it's the never quite the same as being in there in your own right. What was it you learnt about Parliament, once you'd got in, that you hadn't entirely sensed before?

SHORT

I think the drama and the power of standing up and making your speeches. I think it's been limited by so many debates being guillotined, and so many short speeches, but I started to see what you say in a committee or a meeting, and then what you say in the Commons, and finally what you write, is of more and more import. What you write, lastly, because it's there for ever. But making speeches that are recorded in *Hansard* in a kind of dramatic forum: there's a power in it even when you don't get your way. I mean, just saying the truth as you see it is important. It's part of the unwinding of how our society comes to terms with where it's going, I think. So I took it all fairly seriously and spoke fairly often. And in those days, of course, some of the big figures, Denis Healey, Michael Foot, Enoch Powell, would stay in the Commons when they were out of power and come in to the latter end of a debate and make big speeches, and everyone would scuttle back in to listen – that's all gone. Some of that discourse, and debate, and listening, has gone.

HENNESSY

The nature of the tabloid press being what it is, I think you first came to wider public attention because you clashed with the extraordinary Alan Clark about his behaviour in the House of Commons; and also the Page 3 girls in *The Sun*. The nature of the press is that whatever you say about high policy and politics and the condition of people's lives, it's that sort of thing that the media latch on to.

SHORT

Indeed.

HENNESSY

Now it must have been galling for you that this was so. The Alan Clark one, I think you were suggesting that he might have been a little bit squiffy on the night …

SHORT

And he was. I mean, everyone said how outrageous I was to say it. I said, 'I know you're not allowed to accuse people of being drunk, but I do think the Minister has, you know, been imbibing', or something to that effect. In his memoirs much later he said he'd been to a wine-tasting. He was a new Minister, he was a Parliamentary Under-secretary in Employment, he was reading an order about equal opportunities which, of course, wasn't him at all, and was reading in a sneering way, making jokes of it that were very disrespectful. So yes, I got attacked for it, but I don't regret it, and as I say, later he kind of admitted that he had been drinking.

HENNESSY

Tell me about the Page 3 Campaign, the *Sun* Campaign.

SHORT

Well, I stumbled into that again, which is my way. I was in a debate on a Friday about private-members' business and there was Winston Churchill's grandson putting up a Bill that would have outlawed any sexual imagery, any pictures of violence and so on in the media, that really would have outlawed war reporting, sex education – crazy. So I got up and said, 'This is very silly and very dangerous, but if you really want to do something about the dignity of women, I think we should take this Page 3 out of the press, and we can do that without endangering any freedom'. And I hadn't really been aware of the thing, but when you come to the Commons there are these racks of newspapers, and you flip through them when they're having a go at you, and it's really quite stunning how many of those pictures there are. And it does degrade our press I still think; although there's much less of it now, indeed, including *The Sun* giving it up. So, as I spoke, I said, 'I think I'll introduce my own Bill.' And then I got, what seemed like a lot of letters, a few hundred from women, and I'm not aware that it was widely reported, saying 'Please do, please do.' So I did, and then it was thousands, and then it was *The Sun* on my back, wouldn't leave me alone. I still agree with it, and others took it up – but it became a burden, yes.

HENNESSY

You come into the Commons at a time when the Labour Party – well, I think the politest way to describe it is 'engaged in a civil war'. You were a politician of the left, and yet the left, in the eyes of many in the middle ground, was making Labour unelectable. It was a terrible time for the Labour Party, the 1980s.

SHORT

Well, I'm of the left, Attlee left. I'm a Social Democrat of a radical perspective. I'm not a Trotskyist, I never have been. Later, I think it was '87, I was elected to the National Executive and we started to do the reforms of policy, and it became clearer and clearer – I think most of us hadn't understood how all the different Trotskyist groups had come into the Labour Party. And I still really disdain them for their belief in transitional demands, you know, they don't say openly they believe in Revolution, they try to get people to sign up to policies that are unachievable in order to make you into a revolutionary without realising you are doing it. And I really disrespect the dishonesty of that. So I became clearer and clearer about what the problem was; I think lots of us hadn't understood what the problem was. By the time the militants had two MPs in Parliament, they'd started running candidates against us in by-elections. So we had to get those people out, they had to choose the Labour Party or their factions. And I was part of that. It's not nice, but it was necessary to get back to sanity, and an honest Labour Party.

HENNESSY

Neil Kinnock put you on his front bench. What did he ask you to do?

SHORT

Well, it was a shock to me: you get into the Commons and in no time at all they put you on the front bench! But of course, there's hundreds – people don't realise – well, a hundred or so people in positions on the front bench, Whips or whatever, in any government or opposition. So I'd been doing youth unemployment and unemployment before, so I think John Prescott asked me to be a junior spokesman and I did Wage Councils, then I tippled off, I resigned over something, and then I got invited back on to do environmental protection I think, and so on. I took my front-bench responsibilities seriously, but if I disagreed with the party line, I would speak up and tipple off the front bench, and come back again. [*Laughs*]

HENNESSY

A nice verb. I think you tippled off first over the renewal of the Prevention of Terrorism Act in 1988. Now, why was that?

SHORT

Well, I'd been in the Home Office and in the box on the night the Bill was passed, and it had been cobbled together -

HENNESSY

That was on the back of the Birmingham Bombs.

SHORT

Yes, indeed. And my city – my family thought one of my brothers, he used to use that pub and might have been in it, so it was quite close to me, I knew how dreadful it was. But then they'd put together this Bill in that searing reaction to a dreadful event, and there were people in the box with me saying, this is not well thought out. This isn't good legislation. And you remember it was temporary, and it had to be renewed. And then they wanted to make it permanent, you get the escalation. And also there was an element of Neil proving he was a tough guy, and it wasn't considered policy, it was gesture politics and you had to toe the line. Well, these two things offend me. Gesture politics and just having to toe the line to toe the line, rather than be persuaded. So I wasn't persuaded and I didn't.

HENNESSY

Now, your critics might say that you have a penchant for resignation. That in some ways you devalue it – though it's always a great personal step, I'm not in any way diminishing that – by doing it as often as you did. Or were you like Martin Luther, 'I can do no other.'

SHORT

I'm a bit 'I can do no other'; it's not calculated in my case. I don't say, 'Is this going to help my political career or not help my political career?' And I think I was willing and happy to be a back-bencher speaking my truth. I wasn't trying to climb the greasy pole. It's just they kept inviting me up it. So yes, I understand what you mean. I think I'm probably not calculating to a fault. I think maybe one should think about how can you best deploy your influence. I tended to go in, do my work, take it very seriously, but if I was deeply offended by something that was wrong, then I'd walk off, and think that was what I should do.

HENNESSY

It says a lot, that they kept wanting you to come back, doesn't it?

SHORT

I suppose so. But then, as I keep saying, there are loads of people on the front bench. People don't realise how many.

HENNESSY

After Labour's second defeat under Neil Kinnock in 1992, John Smith becomes leader of the Labour Party. I think you had a lot time for John Smith, rated him very highly. And of course he died tragically, just two years later.

SHORT

Absolutely. I didn't support John for the leadership. I supported Bryan Gould, being of the same but more leftist position. Then

John took over the leadership, and he was a man of such comfortable intellectual self-confidence that he didn't have to crush people. He liked having people round the table who put forward ideas, had discussions, and that's of course the politics I like. And I came to really admire and respect him. And I think it's a tragedy for Britain that he didn't survive to become the Prime Minister. I think the '97 Labour government would have been a much more significant, transforming government if John had been the Prime Minister.

HENNESSY

John Smith made you Shadow Minister for Women. He wanted Labour to be a women-friendly party. Do you think something shifted as a result of that? That it did become so?

SHORT

John Smith – I think because of his daughters, and his respect for his wife – he had an instinct that we had to change, and of course Labour hadn't won the women's vote, and the evidence from other countries is that when there's more and more women's participation in the labour market, the voting pattern shifts. So there was what's right and big politics at stake. The only way we could get more women elected was the all-women shortlists which we always twinned with a mixed shortlist in another seat; so we weren't squeezing out men, we were just delivering some women. And we improved our policies in all sorts of ways – domestic violence, childcare etc. And in '97 we won the majority of the women's vote. And yes, he liked me and I liked him. He loved vigorous discussion of policy and so do I. And there's no doubt we would have won under him in '97. Less big majority, but we would have won.

HENNESSY

Some people in the Labour Party said after '97, that under John we wouldn't have won …

SHORT

But that's not true. I mean, this is the 'Pol Pot' New Labour thing; everything started with them. All the basic reforms of the Labour Party had been done under Neil and John to get us back to sanity and electability with some integrity. And the polling was absolutely clear that we were *en route* to win: we had the 'More trusted on the economy', that crucial one. If anyone looks at the evidence, it's not true that we wouldn't have won under John. It is true that Blair, with the purple posters if you remember, and the young attractive family, added more to the majority. Maybe not good, actually. But we would have won under John, there's no question, the evidence is there.

HENNESSY

Am I right in suspecting that there were always one or two things about New Labour that set your teeth on edge, right from the beginning?

SHORT

Yes. Tony and Gordon came on to the National Executive late on. I remember Gordon saying, you have to choose which way you want to make a mark. And there was some argument about reform of the trade-union voting, that perennial chestnut, and Tony adopted some positions, and some positions in the media, that I disrespected profoundly. So I got to know what he was made of, and was not a fan from the beginning.

HENNESSY

Were you worried about the propensity to spin, which you became very critical of later? You talked about people who live in the dark, spinners and so on. Do you think that was a factor from early on in your unease with certain aspects of New Labour?

SHORT

I remember John Smith saying, 'I don't ask my advisers on presentation to tell me what to sell, I want them to help me to sell what I'm in favour of'. And he said, 'I don't suppose people who sell baked beans say, "Should I sell baked beans, or should I sell something else?"' And he was making the point that first you should get some integrity into your policies, and then you should present them as well as you possibly can. I think the spin under New Labour went across that line, and became 'Tell me what you like and I'll advocate it'. And then at some point there becomes little point in being in government … if you don't have any depth and integrity in the message that you're trying to convey, in the policies you're trying to take forward.

HENNESSY

Yet Tony Blair offers you what in many ways, I suppose, might have been your dream job: Secretary of State for International Development in '97, and you did it for six years.

SHORT

Indeed. Well, I was elected to the Shadow Cabinet; he wouldn't have offered it to me otherwise. And obviously he dropped Michael Meacher who was elected to the Shadow Cabinet. But I think it was a judgement that it would cause more trouble to drop me than not. Yes, it was my dream job, and I got really stuck into it and I did it in an old-fashioned way, that is, I respected my civil servants, they respected my leadership, we wrote papers, read them, I got a bigger table in my office, we discussed everything and thrashed out policy, we transformed all the positions of the department, and I was very lucky that at that stage, Number 10 wasn't interested in International Development, unlike, say, Education or Health, where they were telling the Secretary of State what to do. And we developed deeply thought-through, radical policies. We were the leading edge on getting the Millennium Development Goals, to get the whole world to work together to systematically and measurably reduce poverty. We took those from UN conferences. But it was a wonderful experience, a fabulous job, a brilliant department, superb civil servants, and I'm very lucky that my political career included those six years.

HENNESSY

I think also you struck up really rather a good relationship with the Secret Intelligence Service that used to brief you, which might surprise some people.

SHORT

Well, yes. Sierra Leone peace – I was very involved in that. You know it was difficult to understand what that civil war was really about. At first, actually, the successive Cs used to come and see me –

HENNESSY

That's the Chief of the Secret Intelligence Service.

SHORT

Yes, and in the early days their budgets were being cut, this was the end-of-the-Cold War optimism. And I said, well, what do you want me to do? Do you want me to have you spy on governments that I'm working in partnership with? Really, thank you, no! And then along came – maybe I shouldn't name him – and he said you do realise all those presidents ask to see us all the time?

HENNESSY

This is one of the Cs, one of the chiefs?

SHORT

Well, it was one under him.

HENNESSY

Yes, I don't think we want to use his name.

SHORT

No.

HENNESSY

Very charming.

SHORT

Indeed.

HENNESSY

Particularly charming officer, I think.

SHORT

And very well read, and knowledgeable. When I realised that, and he gave me some books to read about Sierra Leone, I thought yes, I want this relationship with these people. After the end of the Cold War, lots of civil wars and conflicts broke out in Africa as the two sides pulled back from every tension on that continent, and that was hurting people and holding back development. And we wanted to do better at ending those conflicts. The Foreign Office didn't care about those conflicts, but they hated me [*laughs*] being concerned about them. But I had a good working relationship with the intelligence agencies, right up to Iraq. But I saw them malfunction around Iraq – getting excited by going with the Prime Minister to the White House, and so on, and lose their way. So I've seen the best and the worst of them too.

HENNESSY

When the question of Iraq begins to make a good deal of the political weather, and the weather inside the Cabinet, the Prime Minister sets up a Ministerial Group on Iraq, which wasn't a proper

Cabinet Committee, if I remember. But you were never on that group. Did you feel that you were deliberately excluded from that inner group of ministers on the run-up to the war in Iraq?

SHORT

You have to know that under Blair the Cabinet did not function as a Cabinet. It became a dignified part of the constitution – I suspect that's still going on, actually, that the Cabinet as it used to be is no longer of significance in the governance in this country. But Blair did everything informally; if he ever thought you were going to say something at the Cabinet that might be contentious, he'd ask to see you first and square it. He was the opposite of John Smith, who liked the discussion and to hear everybody's views. I'm not much bothered with status and so on, and people hovering around Number 10: I'd enjoyed being semi-detached, being able to run my department. But I spoke up in the Cabinet from the beginning, and I thought from the beginning that if we hold on to Blair's ankles he can probably hold on to Bush, and we can probably get a more intelligent policy here. And of course, as you know, you'd have one set of assurances in discussions in the Cabinet and then another set of screaming headlines in the media. I still thought we might be able to avoid rushing to war without thinking through what we were doing, and I tried for that. And there was a lot of duplicity, I'm afraid.

HENNESSY

Did you get a special briefing on the Iraq Dossier, as it became known, in September 2002? The collation, which wasn't done classically by the Joint Intelligence Committee, as these things normally are ...

SHORT

Alastair Campbell never liked me, because of my independence and non-adoration, I suppose, and not always asking his permission to say anything to the media. So when he was in charge of the dossiers I stayed out of them. You can only fight on so many fronts, and I thought, they're just presentational.

HENNESSY

Coming right up to the rim of the war now ... The Cabinet of the 17th of March, when the Attorney General's opinion is brought to the Cabinet ... It's very short, it's very terse by the standards of these things. Did you not feel that, and did you not raise it, at that very last minute?

SHORT

Yes. It was a special Cabinet that I'd asked for. There'd already been rumours in Whitehall that the Attorney General had said there's no clear legal opinion, the military had said they wouldn't go without it. Then he suddenly comes ... Robin Cook's gone by then, he sits in Robin's seat ... He's got this one-and-a-half page typed document, and he starts just reading it. They'd put it round the table, so we all said, 'We can read'. And then I said, but why so late? Have you changed your mind? And things were so tense by then that people were saying, 'Clare, be quiet! Leave it!' So we didn't have any discussion. And it was all very fraught, very last-minute. And now we know it was concocted. And it was drafted as an answer to a Parliamentary question I think tabled first in the Lords, then in the Commons. It wasn't the full legal opinion, or anything like. And he didn't talk about any process of considera-tion, and where his doubts ... there was none of that.

HENNESSY

Did you ask for the longer document that you assumed must be there, that had been made earlier? And indeed, now we know there was one ...

SHORT

No, I didn't know there was a longer document, I was just astonished, and I asked, 'What's happened? Did you change your mind?
How come it's so late?' and they all said, 'Clare, be quiet, leave it,
leave it, leave it.' There was no discussion.

HENNESSY

Do you think you should have resigned at that point? Robin Cook
had gone a day or so earlier, I think.

SHORT

He hadn't gone yet. You know, you booked to give your resignation
speech, and I'd done that, and then I did this radio interview to say,
I'm still thinking that at the last minute, hold on, maybe we can
stop this. And then Blair had me in for repeated negotiations, and I
was thinking, 'We can't stop the war, but we could reconstruct the
country better, and differently'. And there had been careful prepa-
rations in the UN led by Louise Fréchette who was Deputy Secre-
tary-General, all under the radar, and if we could internationalise
the reconstruction I thought we could probably avoid a disaster.
And actually, he promised me that, and of course, it was just to keep
me quiet. But I thought – and this was a big pain for me – I thought
it was utterly wrong to go to war without the UN resolution.

HENNESSY

A specific resolution authorising it ...

SHORT

As promised, as had been promised. And I hadn't then read the
'Project for the New American Century'[2] and that should have

---

2 The founding principles of a neoconservative think tank of the same name.
Its stated goal was 'to promote American global leadership'. Many signatories
went on to serve under President George W. Bush

been circulated in Whitehall, I think it's shocking that it never was. But of course, the Foreign Office wasn't really much in charge either, it was all being run out of Number 10, directly on the phone to the White House and so on. I thought, I'll stay because we can still retrieve what otherwise is a disaster. And it's another of those moments of not calculating my position. But I don't feel bad about it. I mean, it didn't work – but I did it for the best of reasons, and if he had done what he'd promised, I think Iraq would be in a different place today.

HENNESSY

But you'd booked your resignation slot speech in the House of Commons, you got that close?

SHORT

Yes, yes, same day as Robin, I would have come on after him, which would have been quite something, wouldn't it?

HENNESSY

And you don't regret that? Because it would have had a very powerful impact if two of you had gone on the same day.

SHORT

I still think it wouldn't have stopped it. It would have made the vote close – even the vote from the Labour Party was a massive majority. People talk as if that was close. I mean, there was lots of arm-twisting and lots of Labour MPs voted against where their instincts lay. It would have been much better for me. It would have been much happier for me, it would have been better for my political career, but I don't regret it. Of course, I regret it in that the promises he made to me weren't fulfilled, so it didn't have any effect – but I know that I did it for the right reasons, and if he had kept his word – a reconstructed Iraq with big international support and probably the replacement of American and British troops by forces from Muslim countries and so on – it would have been a different Middle East today. So I regret that what I did didn't have any effect, but I'm glad I tried.

HENNESSY

How much later did you go, and what was the reason? What triggered the actual resignation when it came?

SHORT

Well, then it's this promising a UN resolution for reconstruction, which you have to do to comply with international law or otherwise you're not allowed to change the institutions of an occupied territory. They're the breaches of international law in Gaza and the West Bank that goes on to this day with no action. So then I was focused on that, as part of it being absolutely necessary to internationalise reconstruction. And remember Bush came to Northern Ireland, and he said 'UN' about six times and Tony told me, 'Look! Bush is saying UN!' and stuff like that. And then the actual resolution we got was very weak, and the arrangements being made were not to re-internationalise the reconstruction. So I'd completely failed, it was a disaster, and I went.

HENNESSY

There was a lot of attack on you from various quarters, over Iraq and so on. How do you handle attacks, Clare? Are you sensitive?

SHORT

Yes, it hurts, it hurts like ... it hurts a lot. But you know, if you can't stand the heat, keep out of the kitchen. It seems to me these things have to hurt you, to have any sensitivity and concern about what's going on. But yes, it's horrible, I hate it. But this is my Catholic childhood, isn't it? If it's right, you have to do it, whatever the pain.

HENNESSY

You resign from the Labour Party in 2006 and become an independent on the backbenches. Why did you do that? Because that's severing flesh of your flesh?

SHORT

Yes.

HENNESSY

The Labour Party had been part of you for a long time ...

SHORT

Yes. You know, the Catholic Church had been my formation, and then when I decided it was at fault, I gave my heart and soul to the Labour Party, as an instrument of moral advance for Britain and the world. But through Iraq, and then the failure of the party to come clean on it and sort it out and hold to account the lies etc, I thought 'It's lost its way'. And I remember saying to some of my close friends, 'I don't want to lapse again.' That is, you know, what you call Catholics who stop being Catholics. But I did. And actually, I resigned the Whip, but I didn't mean to resign from the Party; but you pay your money to the Parliamentary Labour Party, so if you stop that, it stops your membership. And then I was shocked to find that, even though I'd resigned from the party, I didn't mind.

HENNESSY

Really?

SHORT

Yes, that was the shock.

HENNESSY

You felt so estranged?

SHORT

Yes. You see, I went to a couple of conferences afterwards, and the whole thing's transformed. I mean, you know, there's not much voting, no democratic debate, not much of a fringe. I know the old Labour Party with all the Trotskyist groups in it became screaming and nasty, but the democratic structure of the conference, which is shaped around the model of the Methodist Conference actually, was crucial to a democratic party that brings everyone together with their consent and through debate. That had all gone. And there was no holding to account what had happened on Iraq, and then I thought, 'I don't belong here any more'.

HENNESSY

They must have been lonely, those last four years in the Commons?

SHORT

Yes, indeed. And, you know, I spent nearly 30 years there, and 10 years on the National Executive of the Labour Party. I sort of divorced a lot my friends, really. But I don't regret it.

HENNESSY

Have you not come back to membership?

SHORT

No.

HENNESSY

Not tempted?

SHORT

No. I quite admired and respected Ed Miliband, but no. I think the left is reshaping. The social democrats are in trouble all over Europe. I think we desperately need a change in our electoral system, and then we'd get Greens, SNP, Welsh Nats etc and Labour.

I think we need a pluralised left rather than a party dominated by Blair and Alastair Campbell and everyone having to toe the line and please Mr Murdoch and his papers. I don't like those politics, and I don't think they're good for the country.

HENNESSY

Can I ask you about a story that the public was deeply moved by and loved, which was when you rediscovered your son in the 1990s, who you'd given up for adoption when he was very small?

SHORT

Well, I regretted him being adopted from weeks, months after it happened, after it was done. And I think it's another side of the bad and good of me – I was too rational. It was a rational thing to do, but it was painful emotionally. I was young. And in those days you weren't even on the telephone, I didn't talk to my mother, all that stuff. And I wrote and tried to sort of see if I could retrieve him or see him … There's a system where you can register now, and I did, and lo and behold, he turned up. And I love him to bits, and we're still very close. So, I'm very lucky he came back.

HENNESSY

Wonderful. Looking back over the sweep of your career, what's the greatest satisfaction?

SHORT

My service to my constituency, and all the people that live there, and my respect for them, and my efforts to care for them and represent them. And my six years in International Development – it was the germ of what Britain's foreign policy could be. The way we can make the world safe is to make it more evenly developed, more just, particularly in the Middle East, which is a disaster that's going to go on for years. And the third thing is, using the Commons to speak the truth as I understood it. I'm proud of that, too.

HENNESSY

What's your greatest regret?

SHORT

I really regret that Blair did what he did on Iraq. I think that was a disaster for Labour, and for the world, and for the Middle East. I've got lots and lots – you know, 'Regrets. I have a few'. I mean any serious human being has a lot of regrets, but that's the big one.

HENNESSY

What trace do you think you'll leave on history?

SHORT

I don't know. That's what I think immortality is, everybody leaves scratches behind them, for good and ill, both on the personal level and in the work they do. My international development goes on, and I think that will leave some scratches. I don't know what else. The kind of style of politics that's gone, that might come back? A more honest style of politics? Maybe?

HENNESSY

Finally, if I could grant you one last reform, just like that, wave a wand – what would it be?

SHORT

I'd go for electoral reform to get this pluralisation of British politics that, I think, would lead to a more thoughtful, considered, more progressive, better Britain. Britain playing a better role in the world. I'd go for that.

HENNESSY

Clare Short, thank you very much.

SHORT

Thank you.

Picture Credits

Page 15: Shirley Williams speaking at the launch of the Social and Liberal Democrats party in March 1988.

Page 46: Jack Straw with Tony Blair at Labour Party Conference in September 2004 (© Mike Goldwater/Alamy)

Page 72: Norman Tebbit pictured with Prime Minister Margaret Thatcher at the reopening of the Grand Hotel in Brighton 2 years after it was bombed (© Simon Dack Archive/Alamy)

Page 98: Neil Kinnock addressing an anti-racism rally in Cardiff, July 1978 (© Robin Weaver/Alamy)

Page 120: John Major pictured during the 1997 election campaign (© Mike Abrahams/Alamy)

Page 138: Roy Hattersley photographed on the terrace of the House of Commons (© Aardvark/Alamy)

Page 162: David Steel at Liberal Party Conference at Brighton in September 1977 (© Keystone Pictures USA/Alamy)

Page 185: Margaret Beckett at a coal miners march in Hyde Park, February 1993 (© Doug Taylor/Alamy)

Page 208: David Owen speaking to crowds through a megaphone on the election trail at Sittingbourne in August 1987 (© Trinity Mirror/Mirrorpix/Alamy)

Page 234: Nigel Lawson, on stage with Margaret Thatcher and Geoffrey Howe, receiving a standing ovation at the Conservative Conference in Blackpool (© Trinity Mirror/Mirrorpix/Alamy)

Page 260: Clare Short on the campaign trail before the Welsh devolution referendum of 1997 (© Jeff Morgan 15/Alamy)